DOCTRINES DO GROW

DOCTRINES DO GROW

A Challenge to Believers

Edited by
John T. McGinn, C.S.P.

PAULIST PRESS
New York / Paramus / Toronto

ACKNOWLEDGMENTS

THE MODERN DILEMMA OF FAITH: from *Toward a Theology of Christian Faith*, copyright © 1968 by P. J. Kenedy & Sons. Reprinted with permission.

MYTHS, MEANING AND VATICAN III: reprinted with permission from *America*, Dec. 19, 1970. All rights reserved. © 1970, America Press, Inc.

THE REALITY OF GOD: from *Interpreting the Doctrine of God*, copyright © 1969. Published by Paulist Press. Reprinted with permission.

WHAT DO YOU THINK OF CHRIST?: reprinted with permission from *The Living Light*, Fall 1970. Copyright © 1970 by Our Sunday Visitor, Inc.

CHRISTIAN CONSCIENCE: reprinted with permission from *Guide*, June-July 1967. Copyright © 1967 by The Paulist Institute for Religious Research.

ESCHATOLOGY AS POLITICS: reprinted by arrangement with *New Blackfriars*, a monthly review edited by The English Dominicans at Cambridge, England. This article originally appeared in the April 1968 issue.

THE FUTURE AT BRUSSELS: reprinted with permission from *The Catholic World*, December 1970. Copyright © 1970.

AFTER VATICAN II: reprinted with permission of National Catholic News Service, for whom Cardinal Suenens expressly wrote this article.

Contents

Introduction

MANY DEVOTED, INTELLIGENT CATHOLICS are profoundly disturbed by the doctrinal renewal now underway in the Catholic Church. Their entire previous religious education had firmly convinced them that the Church cannot change—least of all in matters of doctrine. Other Catholics, no less devoted or intelligent, are agitated because doctrinal renewal is so widely misunderstood, suspected and resisted by their fellow believers. One group sees this new focus in theology as a destructive force; the other regards it as necessary, healthy and creative.

I am convinced that these divergent points of view are at the heart of the polarization that causes such bitter skirmishes in this and in other areas of Christian reform. Of course, not everything that marches militantly under the banner of "doctrinal renewal" actually does reflect the authentic teachings of the Gospel. But neither does every strident claim to orthodoxy deserve to be accepted without question. The Church must always keep in balance the twofold obligation: to be true to herself and to renew herself. This applies to every aspect of her life: custom, law, worship, institutions, and even to doctrine.

This slim volume represents the contributions of men who seek to give the current Catholic answer to some of the most fundamental questions of humanity. Alert to the presence and promptings of the Holy Spirit, and responsive to the urgings of Vatican Council II, they aim to foster a better informed and deeper Christian faith. Their answers emerge from an honest dialogue with our present world, with other Christians, and with their fellow Catholics. The hope is that individuals and study groups, even though without specialized training, may come to a deeper appreciation of what the renewal in doctrine is attempting to accomplish.

A word of grateful thanks to the writers, editors and publishers whose cooperation makes this venture possible.

John T. McGinn, C.S.P.
Editor

AVERY DULLES, S.J.

The Modern Dilemma of Faith

FROM THE EARLIEST DAYS all Christian groups have looked upon faith as the indispensable foundation on which the whole life of man before God must be built. "Without faith it is impossible to please him" (Heb 11: 6). Luther ushered in the Reformation with the battle cry, "Justification by faith alone," and the Council of Trent, in its Catholic response to the Reformation, proclaimed that faith is the "foundation and source of all justification." [1] Until recent times Christians debated about the content of faith, but not about the possibility or necessity of faith itself. Today, however, faith as such is widely felt to be problematical. Can a modern man be sincerely convinced that God exists, that he has spoken, and that he says all that the Church attributes to him? If a man questions these things can he still be a believer? Can he be saved?

The situation of contemporary man with regard to faith has been impressively stated by Karl Rahner in

* This article originally appeared as an Introduction to *Toward a Theology of Christian Faith*, Volume V in the series *Readings in Theology* compiled at the Canisianum, Innsbruck, Austria. It contains thirteen other articles to which Father Dulles occasionally refers. Page references, in these instances, are to the original volume. He has recently published *A History of Apologetics* and *The Survival of Dogma*.

4   Avery Dulles, S.J.

a paragraph that might well serve as the text for the present essay:

> Every age has its own task before God; the task of today's world is to believe. For today it is not this or that belief, this or that article of the faith which is called into doubt, but faith itself, man's capacity to believe, man's ability to commit himself completely to a single, unambiguous, demanding conviction. He finds himself in a world changing more rapidly than he can keep up with, a world in which new discoveries are constantly upsetting the world-view he has grown used to. Psychology has discovered unknown depths within him and astronomy has shown him the vast, limitless reaches of the universe outside of him. What new discoveries, what new world he shall find himself in tomorrow he doesn't know. All this is a threat, a challenge, a danger to faith, to man's very capacity to believe.[2]

Conscious of the widespread questioning and confusion with regard to faith, Pope Paul VI on June 29, 1967, inaugurated a "year of faith." In a general audience on June 14, he spoke at some length of the reasons behind this decision.[3] He was fully conscious, he declared, of how difficult it is for modern man to make a sincere and complete profession of faith. Many of these difficulties, he noted, come from the characteristic mentality of our day—that is, from the manner in which men are accustomed to use their cognitive powers. He referred especially to the scientific cast of mind, which employs methodic doubt and admits only what is established by cogent evidence. In order to off-set such difficulties, Pope Paul called for a deeper study of the constitutive elements of faith, and pronounced his blessing on the scholarly work already being devoted to this task.

Convinced of the need of a renewal in the theology of faith, the editors of the Canisianum "Readings in Theology" have selected this subject as the theme of the fifth volume of their series. Thus far, all the volumes in this series have dealt with the fundamental questions of theology, general questions relating to the nature of God's Word and man's response, which must be discussed before the more specialized topics can be treated. Except for the Introduction, all the contributions to this volume are by living theologians from the European continent, and all but one—the Epilogue—are by Catholics. The anthology viewed as a whole gives a fair cross section of the dominant trends in the Catholic theology of faith since about 1950. By and large, the writers show the influence of modern biblical theology and personalistic philosophy. The present introduction is added in order to show the relevance of these European contributions to the current crisis of faith, especially as it appears on the Western side of the Atlantic.

That there should be crises of faith should surprise no one. Faith is inherently at odds with man's fallen nature and with all worldly modes of thought. The world therefore produces crises of faith, just as faith produces crises in the world. Not all crises, moreover, are detrimental. There can be crises of growth as well as crises of decline. Every major social and cultural transition in history has given rise to new crises of faith.

In the past few generations American Catholics as a group have been spared the severe crises that have periodically rocked the faith of Catholics in most European countries and that of many Protestants in the United States. The American Catholic community has been remarkably solid in its belief and religious practice. To some extent the reasons for this are sociological. The immaturity of the Church in this country, while impeding certain desirable developments, forced its members to huddle together for sheer survival and in this way helped to produce a remarkable solidarity.[4]

But the situation of the Church in this country is in rapid flux, so that the problem of faith is taking on new dimensions. The main lines of the historical evolution of American Catholicism in the past generation may be illustrated by comparison with the normal stages by which the faith of the individual passes from childhood through adolescence toward maturity.[5] These stages, briefly sketched in Monden's article in the present volume, have long been familiar to religious psychologists.

The faith of the child is passive and spontaneous. Naturally religious, he seeks a protective environment in which he is surrounded by benign powers. He responds readily to the idea of heavenly forces that take him in their care. In the absence of serious challenges from without, the child is not forced to take a critical attitude toward the contents of his belief. For him, the line between myth and reality, illusion and truth, is blurred. While the ease and simplicity of childlike faith are enviable, such faith is defective insofar as it is normally mingled with superstition and is not yet fully personal and responsible.

Thirty years ago the Church in America existed in a protective situation, not unlike that of the child. The average Catholic was raised in a secluded ethnic group, having its own schools, clubs, and social life. The Church was content to remain a realm apart, without much real communication with the dominant trend of ideas in the outside world. Catholic religious manifestations were characterized by a devout obscurantism, in which awe and wonderment were strongly evoked, and intelligent criticism could scarcely be formulated.

Toward the end of the 1930s Catholicism in the United States entered a new stage. No longer content to be the hereditary religion of isolated ethnic groups in ghetto situations, it began to enter into vital contact with its environment. Thomism became respectable among the intelligentsia, largely through the efforts of the French philosophers Jacques Maritain and Etienne Gilson, who taught and lectured in the United States. Then came the dislocations of World War II, with the draft and military service, which thrust the mass of American Catholics into the mainstream of American life. In the years following the war, Catholic education continued to expand enormously. There were many conversions and abundant vocations to the priestly and religious life. What Ida Görres says of German Catholicism between the two World Wars applies perhaps even more accurately to the United States following World War II:

Quite abruptly, after the war, this "faith of a child" gave way, on a sociological level, to the "faith of youth" in intellectual circles. This was accompanied by appropriate traits of adolescence, manifesting itself as aggressive, triumphant, enthusiastic about theology to the point of intoxication, seeing the real world only through its desires, mistaking the optative mood for the indicative, and believing that the Church, and the Church alone, should have (and had) an answer for everything. All of this involved a kind of alienation from reality in the direction of optimism.[6]

The exuberant vitality of the American Church in these years evokes our admiration, but we must not overlook certain defects—those characteristic of religious adolescence. Catholicism was too assertive, too set on its own values, insufficiently willing to listen and to learn from others. Inevitably, the period of maturity was bound to come; the Church would find it necessary to adjust to the realities of the actual world and in so doing to deepen its own life.

A mature faith is one that has overcome the superficial enthusiasm of youth as well as the naive credulity of the child. Through harsh experience it has learned that evil persists and will persist, that man's ideas and labors, even when well intended, are shortsighted and ambiguous. Faith must lose some of its exuberant self-confidence in order to discover the value of suffering, sacrifice, submission, and to focus its concern upon the God of mystery rather than on tangible values and the exhilaration of specious success.

The present era of American Catholicism may be dated from John F. Kennedy and Pope John XXIII, each of whom, in his own way, summoned Catholics to abandon the alienation of a pretended superiority and to take upon themselves what the Second Vatican Council was to call "the joys and the hopes, the griefs and the anxieties of the men of this age." [7] Instead of standing in judgment on the world, Catholics now began to listen respectfully to it and to study their own past and present deficiencies. They felt obliged, in loyalty to the gospel itself, to expose and overcome everything childish, obscurantist, anachronistic, and corrupt in their own patrimony. While seeking to transform the world according to Christ, they acknowledged the urgency of refashioning their own image of Christ according to the most exigent standards of modern critical thought.

It would be impossible to understand the contemporary crisis of faith without reference to Vatican II, which marks one of the great turning points in the history of Catholicism. For some centuries the Church had adopted a position of increasing isolation from the modern world. Admitting no criticism from within its ranks, and refusing to make any significant concessions to the spirit of the age, it presented an appearance of strength and dignity. Many persons who felt bewildered and disgusted by the flux and ambiguity of modern life turned to the Church as a sure refuge in which the absolute and the eternal seemed most tangibly present. The negative stance of the Church toward modern secularity reached its apex in Proposition 80 of the *Syllabus of Errors* (1864), which condemned the view that the Roman Pontiff can and should reconcile and adapt himself to progress, liberalism, and recent civilization.

But this attitude of aloofness became increasingly difficult to maintain. So all-engulfing are the forces of history that any institution that seeks to immunize itself from them soon finds itself falling behind the times. By disciplinary regulations the Church could perpetuate within its own fold the Thomistic system of philosophy, the Latin language, medieval hymns and vestments, and a monarchical-curial system of government. But as it clung to its medieval forms it appeared to more and more people as antiquated and irrelevant.

Vatican Council II, inspired by the genial leadership of John XXIII, set the Church on a new course.

Instead of condemning the world from a lofty eminence, and denouncing all innovations as defections from the truth, the Church acknowledged its own shortcomings, its sinfulness, and its need for drastic updating. In his Apostolic Constitution convoking the Council, Pope John asked that the Council be "a demonstration of the Church, always living and always young, which feels the rhythm of the times and which in every century beautifies herself with new splendor, radiates new light, achieves new conquests. . . ." [8] In his opening allocution at the first session of the Council he directed that the authentic doctrine of the Church should be "studied through the methods of research and the literary forms of modern thought." [9]

The primary task confronting the Council, according to Michael Novak, was "to insert the Church back into the center of historical life, with respect to the moment of history in which it acts." [10] In many of the Council documents one finds striking evidence of openness to the achievements of contemporary civilization. The Pastoral Constitution on the Church in the Modern World, in its opening pages,[11] assesses the situation of faith in our day by pointing out some of the prevalent spiritual attitudes of modern man—his adherence to scientific method, his confidence in technology, his sense of the growing unity of world history (sometimes called "planetization"), and his dynamic, evolutionary view of reality.[12] In the current ferment of ideas, the Council observes, religion is viewed in a more critical light than before. While in some ways this makes faith more difficult, it has the advantage of purifying religion of the elements of magic and superstition with which it was formerly commingled, and of favoring a more personal and explicit adherence to the revealing God.

In displaying such an openness to secular thinking and to the prevailing mentality of our day, and in accepting their consequences for the life of faith, Vatican II took a courageous step forward, the full effects of which we are just beginning to appreciate. The more we acknowledge the normative value of modern patterns of thought, including critical scientific method, the more exposed and vulnerable our faith seems to become. The Church, including its solemn doctrinal pronouncements, is viewed as historically conditioned. Many Catholics, who previously felt secure under the aegis of an unassailable authority, today feel that there is nothing firm or stable to hang on to. Many would prefer to return to the womb of a protective Church and to reverse, if they could, the effects of the Johannine revolution.

In the wake of Vatican II the Church is teeming with movements of reform and revision. It is torn by tensions between those who are reluctant to part with what seems tried and true and those who wish to sweep away with an angry gesture everything that seems to savor of the past. Practically everyone feels at liberty to criticize the institutional Church from his own point of view. Those who regard themselves as progressive make use of the norms set forth by Vatican II—contemporaneity, relevance, and service—in order to condemn the Church they see before them as outdated, irrelevant, and unprofitable to mankind. Catholics, long accustomed to regard their Church with reverential awe, feel a certain heady delight in their new freedom to protest; but at the same time they are torn by ambivalent feelings. It remains to be seen whether, once they have become used to the new situation, they will be able to maintain a sense of loyal commitment to

the Church, even while disapproving of some of its
practices.

Many of the current difficulties against faith are
directly connected with the present ecclesiological crisis. The youth of today, who feel these difficulties most
acutely, do not wish to be tied to the ideas and values of
a bygone era. The institutional Church, in the eyes of
many, is excessively conservative and concerned for
its own self-perpetuation and aggrandizement. Those
of the younger generation do not want to become the
tools of a gargantuan bureaucracy; they resent being
railroaded into a mass of doctrinal positions the importance of which is by no means evident to them. Per-
sonalistically oriented, they want their faith to
give meaning and fulfillment to their lives in a complex
and confusing world. They want to be actively and
creatively involved, and to experience the joy of community with other persons. Impatiently idealistic, they
are inclined to judge that the Church has conspicuously
failed to meet these needs. An increasing number of
younger Catholics feel only casually related to the
Church as something rather marginal in their lives.

Difficulties of the sort just mentioned, familiar to
anyone who has contact with American youth today,
are evidently not peculiar to the Western hemisphere.
To judge from the contributions of Semmelroth, Rahner, and Monden to this book, similar objections are
raised in Europe. The solution will not come from
books alone, since the difficulties arise out of a wide
spectrum of factors, many of them not primarily intellectual. To gain even a theoretical grasp of the situation—without even addressing oneself to the practical
and pastoral aspects—would involve a study of numerous psychological, sociological, moral, and ecclesiologi-

cal questions far exceeding the scope of a volume such
as this. But the theory of faith, to which we here address
ourselves, has an important role to play. Many of the
articles in this anthology touch on crucial issues such as
the relations between faith and freedom, faith and
community, and faith and the institutional Church.
August Brunner, for example, makes out an impres-
sive case for holding that any true community among
men presupposes some sort of common faith, and that
the deepest community cannot be achieved without a
common religious faith. Thus the Church, as the locus
of common faith, is creative of community. And con-
versely, as several contributors to this work point out,
faith cannot achieve a healthy growth except within
the atmosphere of a believing community, a church.

Many observers are disturbed by a certain indif-
ference toward doctrine, especially among younger
Christians. The complaint is often made that the
Church's teaching conveys an impression of unreality.
In many instances the fault is traceable to poor catechetical techniques. But more fundamentally, it must
be acknowledged that the traditional doctrinal formulations were forged in the light of a general world-
view that has by now become obsolete. By accepting
the modern climate of ideas, Vatican II implicitly
committed the Church to the formidable task of rein-
terpreting its entire dogmatic heritage in such a way
that, as Schillebeeckx says, "its original, unassailable
meaning will begin to function existentially in the
new contemporary self-understanding." Such a reformulation of doctrine is of great importance for the
preservation of the faith, especially among youth:

A clear doubt about representations of the faith which
has not been resolved in the church's confession of faith

as it functions in a proper image of man and the world, can in the long run begin to gnaw away at the church's confession of faith itself,—such as we now see happening everywhere around us in the difficulties of faith with which especially the young are struggling.[13]

As will appear from a perusal of the present volume, one of the notions most urgently in need of re-interpretation is that of faith itself. Many Catholics have been brought up in the tradition of the Counter Reformation catechisms without any real awareness of the historical vicissitudes by which that tradition was shaped. Thus they have accepted the strongly intellectualistic view of faith as an assent to propositional truth, without adverting to the fact that this element was thrust into prominence by the controversies against Lutheran "fiducial faith." So too, Catholics have become accustomed to a sharp contrast between the spheres of faith and reason, looking upon faith almost as if it meant signing a blank check; in this respect modern Catholicism still bears the marks of the struggle against 19th-century Rationalism. Most Catholics, moreover, have been taught to think of faith as something that has come down unchanged from Apostolic times—a notion implanted in great part by the reaction against Modernism at the beginning of the present century.

In recent years Catholic theology has become aware of the dangers in trying to concoct its present doctrine out of magisterial statements made in the course of bygone controversies. The resultant notion can scarcely be a balanced one. It is at least inadequate to describe faith—in the style of many catechisms—as a supernatural virtue by which we believe all the truths which the holy Catholic Church teaches, inasmuch as the Church is the mouthpiece of God, who can neither deceive nor be deceived. As one can see from Schnackenburg's essay in the present volume, this modern notion of faith would have sounded very strange to a first-century Christian. In the early Church faith was not a matter of abdicating one's judgment to an institution, but an enthusiastic response to God arising out of the good news of the gospel.

The very features of faith that were accentuated in opposition to the heresies of the past few centuries have become the greatest stumbling blocks to the modern mind. Rightly or wrongly, our contemporaries complain of "extrinsicism" in the Catholic view of faith. They can make nothing of the idea of a body of religious truth authoritatively imposed upon the human mind from outside. As Blondel observed, the "principle of immanence," holding that all human knowledge must be an actuation of the native powers of the mind, and thus be in some sort produced by man, is fundamental to modern philosophy.[14] The effort of authoritarian thinkers to protect the contents of faith from open enquiry, on the ground that they are guaranteed by sacred sources, can hardly prove successful. The modern secular mind, in defiance of ecclesiastical prohibitions, has progressively extended its critical scrutiny to every area of human knowledge, and claims to have found many faulty statements in the supposedly sacred sources.

The traditional Christian claim that some privileged source, whether Church or Bible, contains the totality of saving truth, is likewise distasteful. Our contemporaries take it for granted that mutually competing systems of thought should correct one another by maintaining a continual dialogue, in which each learns from the others. An unconditional allegiance to any single view of the universe, such as Christian faith seems to demand, impresses the modern mind as fanatical and unscientific. In all other fields of study man is prepared to revise his views as new evidence seems to require. Why should faith be an exception?

Finally, the assertion that divine revelation was complete in the first century of our era seems completely antithetical to the modern concept of progress. History—it is objected—would simply have no meaning if man could do nothing except reiterate a message delivered nearly two thousand years ago. The Catholic Church, while apparently claiming to teach only what was revealed in Apostolic times, today professes a complicated system of doctrine much of which would be unintelligible to the Apostles.

The Church therefore seems to be caught in a dilemma regarding its doctrine of faith. If it continues to resist the infiltrations of modern thought, Catholicism will command the assent of an ever-diminishing band of heroic reactionaries. But if the Church yields to the demands of modernity, it runs the risk of adulterating its own distinctive message and thus of liquidating itself.

While the problem is real and difficult, I believe it can be shown that the opposition between the teaching of the Church and the modalities of modern thought is not so absolute. In opening itself to dialogue with the contemporary world, the theology of faith has much to gain. The apparent conflict is due less to the nature of faith itself—which is equally foreign to the natural propensities of men of every age—than to the fact that the familiar formulations of faith are, as previously stated, conditioned by the controversies of an earlier day. As the contributions to the present volume demonstrate, the theology of faith can be strikingly renewed by contact with the valid tendencies of modern thought.

II

Let us first consider the alleged passivity of faith. Contemporary man is rightly repelled by the notion that faith must be a mere capitulation of reason to a set of statements purportedly delivered from on high. But it seems quite possible, within the bounds of Catholic orthodoxy, to maintain that faith is a human acquisition as well as a divine gift; that the Word of God comes to maturity only insofar as it becomes also the word of man. In the biblical view, the Word of God is something proclaimed by unusually creative human leaders; and on theological grounds it would seem that the creativity of the human mind should not be suppressed but rather enhanced by the grace of God. Revelation occurs when man, under the quickening influence of the Spirit within him, correctly answers the questions of deepest import for his total destiny, his salvation.

Faith and reason are not, as sometimes imagined, mutually exclusive. Faith, as the supreme exercise of reason, arises when the spirit of man, borne by the divine Spirit (see 2 Pt 1:21), overleaps itself. Because human effort is involved, revelation does not come to man easily or all at once. In biblical history, faith is not portrayed as a collection of abstract truths handed to man on a platter. All truth, and perhaps especially "revealed" truth, is a laborious acquisition that takes the cooperation of many minds and the

passage of many years. The Bible records the tortuous
progress of the Judaeo-Christian phylum of revelatory
history over the course of more than a millennium.[15]

Does it seem likely that God has disclosed himself
to none but the biblical peoples? In contrast to the
parochialism of medieval and Counter Reformation
theology, which paid scant attention to the religious
experience of those external to the Catholic Church,
modern man is reluctant to dismiss the other religions
and quasi-religions as simply devoid of revelation. He
takes it almost for granted that faith and salvation
are within reach of all men. He could not believe in
a God who left the majority of mankind without a
ray of heavenly light and grace.

Here again, Catholicism can come to terms with
the modern way of thinking, and in so doing realize
some of the best potentialities of its own tradition.
Vatican Council II has pointed the way. The Decree
on Ecumenism, for instance, makes much of the possibilities of authentic Christian faith in the separated
Churches and ecclesial communities of the East and
West. The Declaration on the Non-Christian Religions
recognizes that not only Judaism and Islam, but even
those faiths untouched by the influence of the biblical revelation, contain reflections of the radiance of
that divine Truth "which enlightens all men" (§2),
and therefore deserve to be met in a spirit of fra-
ternal dialogue and friendly cooperation. The Constitution on Divine Revelation likewise implies that God's
Word comes to men independent of his special historical revelation of himself in the Old and New Testa-
ments. It asserts that God "gives men an enduring
witness of himself in created realities" (§3).

Does God reveal himself in other ways than

through the world's religions, thus making it possible for "non-believers" to make acts of faith? The documents of Vatican II, while not directly answering this question, open up the possibility of an affirmative answer. The Dogmatic Constitution on the Church, after discussing the opportunities for salvation in the various religions, adds that this possibility holds even for the sincere atheist or the conscientious agnostic: "Nor does divine Providence deny the help necessary for salvation to those who, without blame on their part, have not yet arrived at an explicit knowledge of God, but who strive to live a good life, thanks to His grace" (§16). The Constitution on the Church in the Modern World confirms this doctrine by asserting that grace works in an unseen way in the hearts of all men of good will (§22).

In these and similar texts, Catholic theologians find an official recognition by the Church that an act of saving faith is possible without any explicit belief in the existence of God or any religious affiliation.[16] This possibility is very significant for a correct understanding of the nature of faith. If it can exist under these conditions, faith evidently cannot consist essentially in the explicit acceptance of any particular doctrines. While the faith of the professed Christian implies the acceptance of certain revealed truths, such acceptance is not precisely identical with faith itself.

As is generally admitted, the intellectual aspect of faith has been inordinately emphasized since the dominance of Scholastic theology in the high Middle Ages. This deviation was aggravated by the rise of Rationalism, which sought to extend to every field, including theology, the lucidity and precision of geometry. As a result Christianity became so intellectu-

alized that God was sometimes portrayed as a supernatural schoolmaster and revelation as a required
course of study on which one would be rigorously examined at the Last Judgment. The modern mind is
warranted in rebelling against this propositional view
of faith. Man's status before God cannot depend on
knowledge of this kind. Today it is agreed that faith
is not a divinely guaranteed supplement to science
and philosophy, although it is true that the attitude of
faith can direct and energize man's total quest for
self-understanding.

In recent decades the analogy of interpersonal
relations has had a powerful impact on the theology
of faith. Sartre has shown how man, as a free subject,
is in great part responsible for what he becomes. And
Buber makes an important addition when he calls attention to the dialogic aspects of personality: through
personal encounter we are mutually creative of ourselves. In an even deeper sense, according to contemporary theology, man is creatively transformed when he
freely opens himself, by faith, to the God who offers
himself in friendship. Faith is in the first instance a
response to God's interior self-communication in grace.
Only secondarily and derivatively does it involve an
assent to determinate truths that are seen by the light
of grace.

Vatican Council II, in its Constitution on Divine
Revelation, moves away from the Counter Reformation view of faith as a sheerly intellectual assent to
revealed truths. Through his revelation, we are told in
Article 2, "the invisible God out of the abundance of
his love speaks to men as friends." In accordance with
this view of revelation as an offer of friendship, the
Council looks upon faith as personal engagement, in-

volving loyalty and self-commitment. It is an act of the whole man, "an obedience by which man entrusts his whole self freely to God" (§5).

The personalistic interpretation of faith, which may be said to permeate the whole of the present volume, gives unexpected support to a number of the classical theses in the older treatises. For example, it becomes quite evident on this theory why grace is necessary for faith and why faith is necessary for salvation. If faith is in the first instance a responsive openness to the loving presence of God offering himself in friendship, it is obviously the fruit of grace and no less obviously salvific. To accept God's gracious offer is to allow oneself to be taken up, through personal communion, into the sphere of the divine.

Further, this interpretation sheds new light on the traditional doctrine that the motive of faith is the authority of the revealing God. In many presentations the necessity of submitting to the authority of Another appears as an odious restriction on man's free development as a person. But in the newer approach it is evident that the authority of God is not just a particular datum swimming into the range of man's pre-existent apprehensive powers. Rather it is God himself interiorly enlarging the horizons of the human spirit and thus lending new light to the mind. The man of faith does not sacrifice his intellect, or if he does so, he regains it in a fuller way.

But the authority of God cannot be reduced to this intellectual influence. According to the biblical view the Word of God grips the whole man and moves his center of gravity outside himself. It enables him to break away from his own narrow perspectives, to forget himself, and in being spent for others to find himself in a new way. "Whoever loses his life for my sake will find it" (Mt 16:25). Unfortunately, many Christians in our day seem never to have caught this vision of faith. Intent on security in this world and the next, they cling timidly to formulas and rituals and are riddled with fear of "losing their faith." They seem to be singularly lacking in that boldness (*parrēsia*) that characterizes the Christian community in the Book of Acts or the heroes of faith whose praises are sung in the eleventh chapter of Hebrews. Those who do not go outside themselves, risking everything in obedience to God, cannot experience the thrill of finding themselves again in the crucified and risen Christ. They are not, in the full biblical sense, men of faith.

A sound theology of faith can escape the horns of the ancient dilemma between a humanistic autonomy that leaves no room for God and a theistic heteronomy that crushes the authentic development of man. There is such a thing as an "open" autonomy in which, as Mouroux says, "I possess myself, but for another and through another who is more present to me than I am to myself. Faith, it is seen, is always the renunciation of a closed autonomy." [17] Mouroux's "open autonomy" closely resembles what Paul Tillich has described as "theonomy" and Dietrich Bonhoeffer as "Christonomy."

In a personalistic view of faith the status of dogma requires careful attention. The idea that every individual would be bound to assent to all the dogmas of the Church is repugnant to many; yet any other view seems hard to reconcile with what the Church means when it defines a dogma. At least in principle, it would seem that the Catholic would be bound to admit that every dogma ought to be believed. This is not a barrier to my free expansion as an individual, but as Brunner points out in his contribution to this symposium,[18] a necessary corrective to my personal limitations, which would otherwise lead to an unbalanced sectarianism. The universal witness of the Church safeguards the totality of God's revelation. The dogmas express what the whole Church is conscious of having seen by the light of faith.

Whether each individual can bring himself to affirm every dogma with personal conviction is another question. Very often dogmas are phrased in such technical language, or are concerned with such abstruse matters, that the individual may legitimately feel, at a given moment, that some of them are not important or meaningful to himself. Perhaps he cannot accurately understand what the formulas mean. In such a situation he can give at best what Newman would call a "notional," rather than a "real," assent. But if he builds his spiritual life primarily upon those doctrines that he sees as directly and immediately related to the fundamental mystery of salvation, he may in time come to recognize the significance of other, more peripheral but still meaningful doctrines.

The Decree on Ecumenism made an observation of far-reaching importance when it pointed out that "in Catholic teaching there exists an order or 'hierarchy' of truths, since they differ in their relationship to the foundation of the Christian faith" (§11). The individual need not be excessively concerned with compiling a complete inventory, in which every revealed truth would be distinctly listed—assuming that such an inventory were even possible. He would do far better to concentrate on the primary affirmations. Hans Urs von Balthasar, in his article in this collection, rightly declares that "faith is, first of all, the belief that there is absolute love." [19] The gospel might be summed up as the wonderful good news that God offers life in Christ to all men, even though they have done nothing to deserve his offer.

In a former age, when individuality was less pronounced, it was less necessary to distinguish between the types of assent given to different doctrines of the faith. When men believed as members of a Christian family, a Christian tribe, or a Christian nation, faith might more easily be allowed to appear as though it meant adding one's name to the list of subscribers to a generalized dogmatic system. But today the educated believer feels responsible before God for his own faith. If this situation involves the risk that some individuals will, even in good faith, fail to accept the fullness of revelation, it allows for a measure of freedom and responsibility in faith scarcely attainable in earlier ages. Now that it is practically possible for almost any individual to become a non-believer, the faithful are more conspicuously a voluntary elite corps. It is important that they should appear as such. There is nothing more detrimental to the missionary expansion of the Church than the impression that many Christians are groaning under the burden of a belief from which they would rather be liberated.

Within the great Church there has traditionally been, and must continue to be, room for many systems of thought, many temperaments, many human limitations. Not all can be forced to share exactly the same vision. Here as in other matters Vatican Council II has given leadership in the necessary direction. Repudiating the monolithic images of the Church characteristic of the Counter Reformation period, the Constitution on the Church declares that the particular churches "retain their own traditions without in any way lessening the primacy of the Chair of Peter. This Chair presides over the whole assembly of charity and protects legitimate differences, while at the same time it sees that such differences do not hinder unity but rather contribute toward it" (§13). The Decree on Ecumenism applies this flexible notion of catholicity to the differences between the Eastern and Western traditions, and implies that reunion can take place without either's being obliged to forego its own traditional approaches in the understanding and formulation of revelation (§17). It is permissible to see in this text a cautious suggestion that a measure of "dogmatic pluralism" is compatible with communion in the one Church. While "full faith and credit" must be maintained among all churches within the Catholic communion, all need not repeat verbatim the same creeds and confessions.[20]

An increasing measure of diversity, where this is not destructive of the essential unity of the Church, will be a healthy thing for the free and responsible development of personal faith. Such a movement corresponds to a true exigency of our times, and may be expected to progress further than it yet has. As Michael Novak remarks, "Diversity will return to the Church when honesty returns. In a living Church, moreover, diversity is at least as admirable and breathtaking an ideal as uniformity. Nor does diversity destroy unity." [21]

Yet another characteristic of the men of our age, to which we must now turn our attention, is their respect for rational and scientific criticism. In an earlier generation, churchmen sometimes tried to prevent the searchlight of critical thought from being cast upon the Bible and Church history. Religion was cherished as a shelter to which a man could flee without being exposed to troubling doubts. Many in fact turned to the Church to provide an escape from the drab and seemingly meaningless routine of daily life and the barrenness of the secular world. How pleasant to retreat into the "strange new world" of the Bible (as Barth called it), where God was in daily converse with men, where miracles abounded, and where the governing hand of Providence was manifest. No wonder, then, that when the celebrated exegete Rudolf Bultmann declared that the New Testament itself was in need of "demythologization," he was met with cries of anguished indignation. But apart from the term, as controversial as it is ugly, Bultmann has practically won his case.

Nearly everybody recognizes today that the Christians of the first century thought in pre-scientific categories and that the biblical message needs to be radically transposed in order for its true meaning to come home to modern man. To complicate the matter further, theologians are now saying that the thought patterns of Patristic and medieval man were likewise culturally conditioned, and that the whole dogmatic heritage of the Church needs to be critically reviewed before it can be authoritatively stated for modern man. This admission is highly disturbing to those whose concept of faith has been primarily that of an assent to dogmas.

Some feel that honest criticism is a threat to faith. But the opposite is rather the case. If we put our reliance on statements and formulas that are supposedly exempt from rational scrutiny we are constantly haunted by an uneasy feeling that we may in fact be

committed to an illusion. As modern men we cannot
evade the task of thinking critically about our religion.
We must disengage the gospel from every antiquated
world-view and every culturally conditioned ideology. We can no longer look on the world with the eyes
of an ancient Israelite or a medieval Aristotelian, and
there is no reason why we should feel obliged to do so.
A mature faith is humble enough to criticize its own
presuppositions and to learn from the science of its
own day. By continually dying to its own previous
formulations faith plunges ever deeper into the mystery of God.

The temptation to reduce faith to an ideology is
always with us. Just as ancient man wanted to have his
household gods securely in his possession, so modern
man wants to have the content of faith firmly within
his grasp. But faith is never something we can possess
and defend in this way. By its very nature it is a
tenuous type of knowledge. Faith is essentially restless,
forever in quest of understanding, grasped by an object
that exceeds its comprehension.

Because it does not really possess what it affirms,
faith is ceaselessly poised over the abyss of doubt.
In a sense, one may agree with Tillich that faith
harbors doubt within itself—not skeptical but existential doubt. The Catholic Reinhold Schneider wrote:
"There is an unbelief which has its place in the realm
of Grace." Ida Görres agrees and gives a moving description of the "blinded faith" of many Catholics in
our time.[22] To speak of the believer's unbelief, says
J. B. Metz, is not "as some may think, a dangerous
mysticism or intellectual toying with unbelief. Rather
does it lay bare the questionableness of our existence
in faith at any time, and it teaches us to repeat, not in

mere imitation or false pretense, the biblical words: 'I do believe; help my unbelief' (Mk 9:23)." [23]

The greatest threat to faith is not doubt of this kind but rather the wrong kind of certainty. The true unbelievers are the overconfident ones, who think they have fathomed the mystery of life and who prematurely rule out the absolute mystery which is God. When the mind is full of its own certitudes it has no room for God. But one who has accustomed himself to radical questioning, and who realizes the utter insecurity of every human answer, has one of the main prerequisites of faith. The Christian who thinks that his faith is sufficiently protected by philosophy or theology or by any created institution—such a one is really insecure in his faith. Paradoxically, we are not secure until we realize that, humanly speaking, we have no security; that it is God, and he alone, who protects our faith. Only a faith that perceives and accepts its own perilous condition has the true security of living wholly off God. "Unless you accept God as firm, you have no firm place to stand" (Is 7:9).[24]

One final aspect of the modern mentality, already indicated above, demands further discussion here because of its repercussions on the doctrine of faith. Men today, especially those of the younger generation, are oriented more to the future than to the past. They spontaneously doubt the adequacy of any idea or institution handed down from earlier times, and are consequently loath to admit that right doctrine consists in repeating what was said by previous generations. They are exhilarated, however, by the idea that we have a great new world to build, intellectually and spiritually as well as materially. Whereas our ancestors took it for granted that the Golden Age lay somewhere in the remote past, modern man is convinced that it still lies ahead and that he has a responsibility to contribute to its realization.

On some presentations, faith would appear to be a commitment to the past rather than to the future. Revelation is asserted to have reached its completion in Christ, or at least by the end of the Apostolic age. Since then, there is nothing to do but to repeat what was then good news, but scarcely deserves to be called news any longer. The gospel therefore becomes increasingly trite. Must we always speak as though salvation history ended with the Apostles, so that God has nothing more to say to us through the history of our times?

Vatican II, stressing contemporaneity as a value, was sensitive to this problem. As against various static images of the Church which had become prevalent since biblical times, the Council resurrected the biblical and Patristic image of the Church as God's people, still on pilgrimage toward the Promised Land.[25] While stressing that God's self-revelation reached its unsurpassable fullness in Christ, the Council left ample room for development in the Church's assimilation of that fullness in new and unpredictable ways. Without using the term "continuing revelation," Vatican II allowed for something of the kind. Echoing a favorite term of John XXIII, it spoke repeatedly of the need to discern "the signs of the times" through which God continues to address his people.

The Church, according to the Constitution on the Church in the Modern World, "labors to decipher the authentic signs of God's presence and purpose in the happenings, needs, and desires in which this people [of God] has a part along with other men of our age" (§11). Portraying divine tradition as a dynamically developing patrimony, the Constitution on Revelation assures us that by means of tradition "God, who spoke of old, uninterruptedly converses with the Bride of His Beloved Son" (§8). Thanks to this process, the Church unceasingly discerns new aspects of what previously lay hidden. "The Church constantly moves forward toward the fullness of divine truth until the words of God reach their complete fulfilment in her" (*ibid.*).

We may, and should, continue to speak of a "deposit of faith." Faith, as an encounter with God who meets us from out of the future, is an event that has occurred, and has left its traces in history. The Church cherishes the memory of God's previous self-manifestations, and especially that of his irrevocable self-giving in Jesus Christ. These tokens of God's love and fidelity, however, are not to be clung to for their own sake. Their chief value is to nourish our trust that God continues, and will continue, to give himself until we see him "face to face." Faith as a partial and progressively deepening anticipation of the final vision is totally in tension toward that which is to come. The commitment of faith, therefore, does not shackle us to an infancy that we should be outgrowing. On the contrary, it beckons us forward "to mature manhood, to the measure of the stature of the fullness of Christ" (Eph 4:13).

Men sometimes speak as though faith were a thing of the past, or were dying out. Because men are fickle, they are always falling away from the true faith, and the prospects of faith are always dim. But because God is loyal to his covenant promises, faith is always being rekindled in the hearts of men, and its prospects are always bright. The forms and expressions of faith may vary, but faith itself never ceases to be accessible. Since God is man's absolute future, and since he continually draws men to himself, we may confidently assert that faith too has a future.

NOTES

1. Session VI, chap. 8; Denzinger *Enchiridion symbolorum,* ed. A. Schönmetzer (Freiburg, 1963), 1532 (= 801).

2. "The Faith of the Priest Today," *Woodstock Letters* 93 (1964), 3–10, p. 5; reprinted in *Philippine Studies* 13 (1965), 495–503; German original in *Orientierung,* §§19 and 20 (1962).

3. *Osservatore Romano,* June 15, 1967, p. 1.

4. See Will Herberg, *Protestant-Catholic-Jew* (New York, 1955).

5. I recapitulate here some thoughts already sketched in my note, "Faith Come of Age," *America,* August 5, 1967, p. 137.

6. Ida F. Görres, "The Believer's Unbelief," adapted by A. Z. Serrand, *Cross Currents* 11 (Winter, 1961), 51–59, p. 53.

7. Pastoral Constitution on the Church in the Modern World, §1. In citing this and other documents of Vatican II, I follow the translations edited by Joseph Gallagher in *The Documents of Vatican II,* ed. W. M. Abbott, S.J. (New York, 1966).

8. Text in Abbott, *op. cit.,* p. 706.

9. *Ibid.,* p. 715.

10. *The Open Church* (New York, 1964), p. 70.

11. Especially §§5–7; see Abbott, *op. cit.,* pp. 203–205.

12. These factors correspond closely to those singled

out by Monden in the present volume; see *infra,* pp. 229–34.

13. E. Schillebeeckx, O.P., "Faith Functioning in Human Self-Understanding," in *The Word in History,* ed. T. P. Burke (New York, 1966), pp. 58–59.

14. One may observe the workings of Blondel in Muschalek's discussion of faith and faith's certitude, in the present collection, *infra,* pp. 186–92.

15. Man's role in the revelatory process is brought out by Rahner in his essay, "Observations on the Concept of Revelation," in K. Rahner and J. Ratzinger, *Revelation and Tradition,* trans. W. J. O'Hara (*Questiones Disputationes* No. 17; New York, 1966); German original: *Offenbarung und Überlieferung* (Freiburg, 1965).

16. See here especially Karl Rahner's essay, "What does Vatican II Teach about Atheism?" *Concilium* 23 (1967), 7–24.

17. See *infra,* p. 103.

18. See *infra,* pp. 258f.

19. See *infra,* p. 128.

20. See G. Dejaifve, S.J., "Diversité dogmatique et unité de la révélation," *Nouvelle Revue Théologique* 89 (1967), 16–25, and, more briefly, my note, "Faith and Dogmatic Pluralism," *America,* May 13, 1967, p. 728.

21. *Op. cit.,* p. 358.

22. *Art. cit.,* p. 57.

23. "Unbelief as a Theological Problem," *Concilium* 6 (1965), 73–74. Monden deals with the same problem when he makes a distinction between a question within faith and a doubt of faith; see *infra,* pp. 213–17.

24. I owe this rather free translation, which preserves the play on words in the Hebrew, to an oral suggestion made by J. L. McKenzie, S.J. In his contribution to the present volume Muschalek also makes use of this passage (p. 175). Drawing from a wealth of Scriptural witnesses, he carefully distinguishes faith's certitude from mathematical-scientific certitude and all other forms of inner-worldly security. See *infra,* pp. 172–86.

25. See Constitution on the Church, §8.

ANDREW M. GREELEY

Myths, Meaning and Vatican III

ENOUGH YEARS HAVE PASSED since the close of Vatican II for us to be able to state with some confidence what happened in the Council and what did not happen, what tasks the Council successfully accomplished and what challenges remain to be wrestled with in the remaining decades of the 20th century.

It seems to me that there are four principal accomplishments of the Council:

1. The fixed, immutable, unquestionable structure of the Church's organization and theory that had persisted for centuries was definitely opened up. The symbol of Pope John's wide open window, never to be closed again, is reflected in the Constitution on the Church, which represented a decisive turning away from the juridical and apologetic approach to the Church that had been typical of most of Catholic theology for several centuries.

2. The principle of collegiality provided the Church with an organizational theme which, on the theoretical level, can serve as the basis for profoundly

* Reverend Andrew M. Greeley is a program director of the National Opinion Research Center at the University of Illinois (Chicago Circle). He has written extensively for scholarly and popular journals and is the author of numerous books in the fields of sociology and religious affairs.

changing the routinized patterns of behavior that had given shape and form to the Church for several centuries. Even if the Church organization of the future has not yet come into being, at least the principle is there according to which it can begin.

3. With the Pastoral Constitution on the Church in the Modern World, Catholicism officially opened itself up not merely to the possibility of dialogue with separated brother Christians, but to the whole vast culture that we call the modern world. Science, technology, political democracy and humanism were no longer things to be wary of and to warn the faithful against. They now represented basically benign influences whose defenders and practitioners could be treated as sincere men of good will.

4. The Constitutions on the Church and on Divine Revelation created the beginnings of a theological context within which Catholicism could address the modern world and also address its own membership to the extent that the membership is deeply involved in the modern world.

These accomplishments, while they represent only beginnings, ought none the less not to be minimized. For if they are only beginnings, they are at least good beginnings. But it would be a serious mistake to pretend that they are more than that.

There were, on the other hand, three "major" failures of Vatican II, though in the nature of things it certainly would have been too much to expect that the Council could cope with the sorts of problems implied by these failures.

1. Even though the Constitution on the Sacred Liturgy was a beautiful theoretical document, it did not address itself to the most critical problem—its own

implementation. It assumed, quite naively from the point of view of the sociologist, that it was possible to achieve the goals of liturgical renewal through the existing parish structures. There have been many criticisms of the failure of the new liturgy to produce all the happy effects that it seemed to promise. Most of the criticisms have focused on the erratic and frequently unpredictable modifications that have been made, it seems, almost every year since the end of the Council. Many bishops and priests have argued that the "people" are confused. In fact, however, the people do not seem to be all that confused. One is afraid, rather, that the bishops and clergy in question are engaging in what psychiatrists call projection.

It is unfortunate that the changes could not have been introduced all at once. It is unfortunate that better educational programs did not accompany the changes. It is even more unfortunate that the liturgy became a political football in the ongoing battles between the progressives and the conservatives of the Roman Curia. But the real problem of liturgical renewal is not the pace and direction of the modification of ceremonies, particularly since in many countries the ability of the Congregation on Rites or a national episcopal conference to control liturgical change has practically vanished. The real problem has been that the liturgy, which is clearly designed to celebrate intimate community, becomes quite meaningless in a large Sunday congregation where there is no intimate community. Turning to one's neighbor just before communion, shaking hands with him and wishing him peace is a pleasant exercise. But if one's neighbor in church happens to be a stranger before the "handshake of peace," he is also a stranger after it. Liturgical ceremony does not create intimate community. On the contrary, it celebrates it and reinforces it. Presumably, Vatican Council III, which one trusts is convened at least before 1975, will address itself to the critically important question of the structure of the local worshiping community. Until this question is handled, liturgical renewal is doomed to be substantially less than a success.

2. While the intentions of the Pastoral Constitution on the Church in Modern World were certainly excellent, its sociological and economic assumptions are at best naive. (The Church's continuing failure to demonstrate any more than passing concern about the world's population problem is, of course, intolerable.) It is essentially a sociological document written by men who, it is much to be feared, are sociological amateurs. Their basic assumption of a unidirectional, continuous and genetic social change involving progress from the sacred to the secular is simply unacceptable. (And the watered-down Marxism of Fr. Jean Lebret in *Populorum Progressio,* the encyclical on development, should, I think, be unacceptable to most students of world economics.) The survival of the primordial and the ethnic in an industrializing world, despite all predictions to the contrary, confounds some of the most basic assumptions of the naive sociology that went into the Constitution. It is to be hoped that Vatican III, in addition to addressing itself with the most serious urgency to the population problem, will take a much more careful look at the complexities of the modern world.

3. Nor was any real attempt made at Vatican II to develop catechetic styles for presenting the Good News of the Christian faith in modern times. Perhaps this failure was inevitable because the Council was in

effect the beginning of a theological revival and not
the maturation of one. Unfortunately, in the absence of
an appropriate catechetical style, the problem of edu-
cating or re-educating the Catholic population to the
rather different Church that emerged after the Council has become most serious. In the English-speaking
world, at least, a grave disservice has been done to
many devout Catholics. They were raised with one
vision of the Church as an essentially fixed, immutable
religious form; they found themselves suddenly trans-
ported into a very different vision of the Church in
which change, growth and openness were emphasized. While, by and large, they seem rather pleased
with the new Church, it must be said in all candor
that little attempt has been made either to explain the
reason for the change or the theology which permits
us to assert that a changing Church is a more desirable
Church than an immobile Church. Their confusion is
not so much over the new liturgy, or the vanishing
of Friday abstinence and St. Christopher; their confusion is over *the* critical Christian question, which,
incidentally, is not, "What must I believe?" but
rather, "What should I believe?"

It often seems, in fact, that the papacy, hierarchy
and clergy are so concerned with working out their
own identity crises that they have forgotten all about
the laity and are quite incapable of hearing the rising
demand for religious meaning that the laity are making.
It is much to be hoped, therefore, that Vatican III
will be in fact what Vatican II claimed to be: a pastoral
council, that is to say, a council concerned about the
reformulation of the Gospel message, so that it does
represent something meaningful to a Christian laity
ever more desirous of religious meaning.

One must comment in passing on the extraordinary

shallowness of much that passes for reform in religious education at the present time. Many of the so-called practitioners of religious education have seemed more interested in telling people what they could not believe any longer than in presenting the core of Christian belief. It seems frequently that a course or two in summer school sessions, or perhaps a year in a "religious education" program, has persuaded many religious educators that they are in fact theologians. Some of the most incredibly naive psychological, sociological and pedagogical nonsense has masqueraded as solemn theory for religious education; and almost each year a new catchword or a new gimmick is advanced with far more confidence than humility as *the* answer to the catechetic problem. Perhaps the most popular of these "answers" has been the so-called "salvation history" school of catechetics, which, incidentally, is frequently a very much watered down and simplified version of the salvation history approach of Scripture analysis. A whole generation of religious educators have gone forth dogmatically convinced that salvation history was *the* answer. It of course turned out not to be the answer at all, a result that led some religious educators to leave the priesthood and religious life, others simply to deny the facts and proceed blindly ahead with their salvation history as a technique, and yet others to search for another prepackaged magic answer.

The search for prepackaged answers promulgated by "experts" seems to be an unavoidable phenomenon of the post-Vatican Church as many immature personalities attempt to replace a discarded collection of certainties with a brand new collection of certainties. There have been far too many "experts"— whose credentials, incidentally, generally leave much

to be desired—who have been only too willing to appear on the scene with such certainties. It is to be
hoped, therefore, that Vatican III be concerned not so
much with prepackaged catechetical programs as with
a new style of religious education that does facilitate
the Church's response to the religious needs of man in
the modern world, needs that—despite the dogmatic
proponents of secularism—are every bit as strong as
they were at any other time in human history.

I should like, therefore, to make a "modest suggestion" for consideration at Vatican III. Taking my
lead from a point made by Paul Ricoeur, in his
Symbolism and Evil, I would suggest that our concern ought to be with "the interpretation of myths."
Religion, I assume, is a "meaning system"; that is to
say, a series of responses to the most basic and fundamental questions a man can ask. What is the nature of
the real? What is the purpose of human life? Does
good triumph over evil or evil, good? Is reality gracious
or hostile? Does life triumph over death or death over
life? How does the good man live? I further assume
that no man is without a meaning system and that the
symbol "God" is a convenient way of summing up our
answers to these fundamental religious questions. I
finally assume that, while a man may use any set of
symbols, from symbolic logic to Aristotelian philosophy,
to express his answers to the religious questions, the
normal way most men have used has been their sacred
story or the myth.

In many Catholic circles the use of the word
"myth" creates a great deal of discomfort, for myth
is assumed to be something that is "not true," or a
fable, or a legend, or a pious fairy story. In fact, of
course, this is not the way myth is used by most con-

temporary students of mythology. A myth is rather an interpretation of the meaning of reality, something that the myth-maker perceives as very true indeed; far more true than a simple historical narrative. We do not have in the myth a video-tape "instant replay" of historical events; we have, rather, a profound and serious attempt to interpret the meaning of the events. Myth is used in the same way that St. Paul uses the word "mysterion," a reality which purports to reveal an even greater reality. The Resurrection, for example, is a myth. This is not to say that it is false, or that it is a fable, or that it is not an historical event. Beyond all question the early Christians had a profound experience of Christ after His death. There is no other conceivable explanation of the enthusiasm with which they committed themselves to the spread of Christianity. An attempt to explain the precise nature of this post-Crucifixion experience of Christ is, of course, very important, but if one does not get beyond the theological explanation of the "how" of the Resurrection to the "what," one has sadly missed the point.

But the most important question that can be asked about the Resurrection is: "What does it symbolize?" That is to say, what does the Resurrection tell us about the ultimate nature of reality? The Christian response to this question is, of course, one of the most staggeringly optimistic responses that man has ever offered. For the Christian says that the Resurrection symbolizes not only the triumph of goodness over evil, not only the triumph of one man over death, but also the fact that *all* men will eventually triumph over death. If Christianity is to be rejected, one ought to reject it not simply because one believes it impossible for one man to rise from the dead, but because one believes it absolutely absurd and incredible that all men should rise from the dead.

This, then, is the common and ordinary way that man has used to express religious truth. A myth is simply a symbolic story, one that is frequently told by being enacted in a ritual. Alan Watts describes a myth as "a complex story, some no doubt fact and some fantasy, which for various reasons human beings regard as demonstrations of the inner meaning of the universe and of human life." According to Watts, in *The Two Hands of God,* the "meaning is divined rather than defined, implicit rather than explicit, suggested rather than stated." He adds: "The language of myth and poetry is integrative, for the language of image is organic language . . . the mythological image is what gives sense and organization to experience."

In a companion volume, *Myths of Creation,* Charles Long argues: "Myth . . . points to the definite manner in which the world is available for man. The word and content of myth are revelations of power." Myths integrate man's total life experience and interpret it for him. They go both higher and lower than scientific propositions.

Mircea Eliade, the greatest among the students of what used to be called comparative religion and now is called history of religions, in his *Patterns in Comparative Religion,* observed: "What we may call symbolic thought makes it possible for man to move freely from one level of reality to another. Indeed 'to move freely' is an understatement; symbols . . . assimilate and unify diverse levels and realities that are to all appearances incompatible."

For most men in the course of human history the telling and retelling of the religious myth was enough.

It was not necessary to analyze and explain the myth. The myth itself provided in an implicit and poetic fashion the response to man's fundamental religious questions. But in our day, for three different reasons, the myths must be interpreted.

1. A superficial science assumed that myths were meant to be history in the same sense that modern scientific history is, and therefore they summarily rejected them as fables. Even though more modern research on mythology has passed beyond such simpleminded reaction to myths, the simpleminded reaction still permeates the educational systems of the Western world. It is therefore necessary to explain patiently what mythology is all about.

2. The myth is a poetic approach to reality. Apparently one of the prices we have had to pay for progress of science, or at least for an educational system dominated by positivism, is that our poetic sense is snuffed out rather early in life. We are led to believe that there is only one valid form of knowledge—scientific reasoning—and only one valid form of expression —the language of scientific reasoning—hence, any other modality of thought and expression, and especially that which is basically poetic, is viewed with suspicion and distrust. Even though the current epistemological revolution is asking devastating questions of the positivist assumptions, these assumptions still reign supreme in Western educational circles.

3. Contemporary man has developed to a much higher level of competency than any of his predecessors the powers of abstract thought. He therefore is almost incurably driven to ask the question: "But what does it mean?" To enjoy a passage of poetry, for example, he must puzzle out its meaning. Then, un-

derstanding the meaning behind the poetic imagery, he can, at least on occasion, enjoy and appreciate the imagery.

The first two reasons for the necessity of explaining myths are unfortunate and may pass with time. The third reason, however, is one that ought not to be evaluated negatively. Much of the tremendous scientific and technological progress, as well as much of the understanding of human nature on which our great world civilization is built, is rooted in the human propensity to ask why. There is no reason, one suspects, that that propensity need weaken man's capacity to exercise poetic modalities of knowledge and expression. Quite the contrary, it seems altogether likely that the poetic instincts can reinforce scientific reason and vice versa.

If my assumptions are correct, what is required is not, despite Rudolph Bultmann to the contrary, an exercise in demythologizing. It is rather an exercise in explaining and interpreting the myths; that is to say, in expressing in propositional form the religious truths which the myths embody.

In a forthcoming book I shall attempt in considerable detail to engage in myth interpretation. For the moment, it suffices I outline what I consider to be the six central myths of the Christian faiths and indicate the implications of these myths as man's answers to the basic religious issue:

1. Yahweh the covenanter: Unlike the gods of the neighboring peoples who either had to be placated or awakened from sleep, the God of the Jews made a firm and irrevocable commitment to His people, a commitment from which He would not turn away, no matter how great their infidelity. This symbol repre-

sents the Israelite conviction that Ultimate Reality was fundamentally good.

2. Yahweh the jealous lover (particularly as described in the Book of Osee): This symbol of the Ultimate Reality pursuing His beloved people as a man would a wife whom he was desperately in love with despite her infidelity represents the Jewish conviction that Ultimate Reality is not only gracious but loving; indeed, passionately, almost blindly, loving.

3. Yahweh promising a messianic age: The messianic mythology of Deutero-Isaiah and of the Book of Daniel symbolizes the Israelite faith that, in the final analysis, good will triumph over evil and eliminate evil from the world.

4. The combination, particularly in St. Mark's gospel, of the myth of the Son of God with the myth of the Suffering Servant. This represents, according to Paul Ricoeur, the most profound of the Christian insights. For it is the Christian conviction that Yahweh fulfilled His promise to bring in the messianic age, in which evil would be conquered by good, precisely by sending His Son as the Suffering Servant. In other words, the Resurrection was made possible by the Cross. Life triumphs over death, but only first by dying.

5. The Eucharistic myth: In this Jesus gathers His band of brothers—His happy few—around a family banquet table, proclaims His unending friendship with His followers, urges them to be friends to one another, and instructs them to continue the banquet as a sign in the cause of friendship. The Eucharistic myth says that the Ultimate Reality not merely loves us so much as to become a Suffering Servant for us, but now proclaims us to be His friends and urges us to bear witness to His Good News by the quality of our love. "By this

shall all men know that you are my disciples; that you have love one for another."

6. The Spirit myth: The Spirit is the dancing God of Pentecost. Ultimate Reality comes in fire and wind to move men to religious enthusiasm, to stir them to the depths of their souls in the service of the Good News. I take it that the Pentecostal myth represents the Christian conviction that the Really Real has decided to be dependent on us for completing the messianic age begun with the Death and Resurrection of Jesus. The Spirit comes precisely to stir us with enthusiasm for the messianic mission.

It seems to me that the specifically Christian myths described above are particularly pertinent to the religious problems of the modern world. For, as Brian Wicker has observed, modern humanism with all its admirable emphasis on human self-fulfillment comes apart in the face of the ugly reality of death. In Wicker's words, "the Christian is merely the humanist who is sure of the ground on which he stands." Furthermore, the Eucharistic myth responds to the search of contemporary man in a polarized world for the conviction that friendship between man and woman, young and old, rich and poor, black and white, is possible. Finally, the Spirit myth reassures modern man, so desperately concerned about personality development, that there is after all some ultimate purpose behind the quest for self-fulfillment.

It will be seen that what I am urging here is an approach to the proclamation of the Christian message that asks what the imagery of the Christian tradition provides in the way of answers to man's fundamental religious needs, for meaning and for community, which all men have experienced in every society that the world has ever known. My argument obviously is in direct disagreement with those who hold that modern man needs no ultimate scheme of interpretation, that he has long since lost the capacity to experience the sacred and the mythological. My strategy is the exact opposite of Bishop James Robinson's, for example, who would have us present to the modern world a thoroughly demythologized Christianity. I can only observe that the good bishop's strategy does not seem to have been very successful at winning converts, perhaps because, like so many other clerics, the bishop thinks that the myth is a fable or a fairy tale. The modern world wants no part of fables, one supposes, but it very much wants explanation, meaning and community. Christian catechesis that is conscious of the really desperate nature of the meaning-search at the present time might be an extraordinarily effective means of proclaiming Good News that is both good and new.

CHARLES N. BENT, S.J.

The Reality of God

FOR MANY IN THE modern world, the reality of God
has become blurred, dimmed or completely eclipsed.
Traditional concepts of God have lost all relevance and
meaning for a large number of people. Both secular and
religious men have experienced the absence of God
in the modern world. But despite the many truly
absurd features of human existence, the religious believer remains convinced that there is an ultimate solution to the problem of man, an answer rooted in the
unfathomable mystery of God. He remains convinced
that God is able to draw meaning out of chaos and
that the power of evil will eventually be overcome.
He remains confident that mankind will regain the
capacity to see God involved in human affairs.

During the past one hundred years man has
finally come to recognize his proper place in the evolutionary scheme. His interests have shifted from the
cosmological sphere to the anthropological, a shift
which has occasioned a flood of new questions regarding the nature of man and his relation with God. Much
of the current debate concerning the Death of God and
secularity is rooted in this shift in emphasis. For the
religious believer, the question of man draws one to

* Father Charles Bent is the author of *The Death of
God Movement,* has taught Sacred Scripture at Holy Cross
College, and is engaged in graduate study at Yale Uni-
versity.

the threshold of the question of God. Man's transcendence allows him to be open to the revelation of God, to stand before the infinite God as a possible recipient of a divine revelation. Man finds himself immersed in a vast mystery which he cannot comprehend adequately. The Christian believer is convinced that the unknown God has disclosed himself to man, the hearer of the word. God's revelation has come to man in history. The Christ-event represents God's definitive word to man. According to Christian theology, that word must be accepted even when the prevailing mood is not receptive to it, since the revealed word is not subordinate to modern consciousness. Relevance is always a legitimate and necessary concern of the Christian, but it is not the ultimate norm of religious truth.

All of man's images of God are tied to this world. Even revealed concepts of God are thoroughly human concepts; they must be if they are to be understood by man. But they are also more than human concepts when viewed from another frame of reference; they point beyond themselves to the infinite mystery of God. Even in revealed religion, then, man's knowledge of God is indirect, analogous, oblique and incomplete. God is disclosed to man as Totally Other, as ineffably above all else that exists and can be conceived. Man's knowledge of God, therefore, is essentially negative rather than positive.

Modern man's experience shows him that God is not the world. God is completely Other than man or the world, but man's concepts of God remain anchored in culturally determined thought forms. The absence and silence of God in the modern world provide a clear indication that God is not of this world. Contemporary man's experience of God shows that God does not belong in the concept of the world; instead, he is found to be the infinite presupposition of the world. God, then, is a known unknown. He is not just another object in the field of the known. The God who corresponds to the object of religious belief is not the God of the philosophers. The hypothesis of God is an existential possibility, not the final step in a long line of syllogistic reasoning. The absolute ground of being and intelligibility has revealed himself to man who is spirit in the world and hearer of the word.

While God is disclosed as Wholly Other, he is not limited to this manifestation. The Christian believer confesses a God who is both transcendent and immanent. It is unfortunate that western man has learned to view transcendence almost exclusively in spatial terms. Too frequently, God's transcendence is understood in terms of distance and remoteness, while immanence is viewed in terms of closeness. History shows that this bipolar relationship has frequently collapsed into one or the other pole in man's ceaseless attempt to understand the divine. The Christian believes that the Wholly Other reality of God is actually present to man in the events of human history. Man is immersed in the unfathomable and incomprehensible mystery of God. Transcendence, therefore, should be viewed in terms of otherness rather than in spatial terms, and immanence should be understood in terms of a dynamic personal presence rather than in terms of physical proximity.

The task facing the modern Christian is to fashion meaningful concepts of God while clearly recognizing that all human conceptions in this realm are only pointers and indicators of an underlying infinite mystery which completely eludes man's grasp. Man finds himself on the edge of a great mystery which he is incapable of comprehending adequately. The visible appearance of God in Jesus of Nazareth points to the primordial reality of the infinite invisible God; it orients man in the proper direction.

The Christian believer denies certain conceptions of God. God, for him, is much more than just the ultimate objectification of man's inward human experiences; he is more than a supreme symbol of man's self-understanding or an ideal focus of all human aspirations. He is disclosed as being totally beyond finite being and not just another object on the horizon of knowledge. Moreover, the God of divine revelation is not the God of theistic metaphysics.

No one who makes the statement 'I believe in God' can offer a fully adequate explanation of what he precisely means by that statement. Its full import is never grasped completely, even by the one making the statement; many uncertainties and ambiguities are included in it. With the passage of time and after much effort, under the providence of God, a man can come to a more explicit realization of what is actually meant by such a statement, but he will never reach an adequate comprehension. Man's understanding of God's nature is negative rather than positive; it is easier, in other words, to know what God is not than to know what he is. Admittedly, much of what passes for orthodox Christian belief today is actually superstition, although it is not intended to be such, and many worship a false god made in the image and likeness of man. But the true Christian confesses the God revealed in the person of Jesus of Nazareth and earnestly tries to discover the full meaning that the Christ-event has for man.

Against the background of increasing anthropological concerns, two possibilities emerge as alternative commitments: theistic or atheistic humanism. Modern man is faced with the option of choosing either religious or secular humanism. Each individual must choose one or the other alternative. But, as one theologian has recently pointed out, this choice is not entirely a private affair. This decision for or against God reflects a high degree of corporate responsibility. Such a choice must be made in the light of one's solidarity in the human condition. A man's choice for or against God has consequences which transcend his own private sphere of interests and concerns.

If modern man is to arrive at a mature understanding of the true nature of Christian belief, then he must learn to develop an authentic humanism in addition to an authentic theism. Unfortunately, humanism is too frequently placed in polar opposition to religious theism. A distinction should be made between secular humanism and humanism. While it is true that the Christian denies that human values are absolute, too many forget that they are still values and should be recognized as such. It is wrong to magnify man out of due proportion, but it is equally wrong to minimize the dignity and grandeur of man. Since the human being is the only valid symbol of God in the world, Christians must strive to develop a true Christian humanism and a viable theology of the secular. Only by loving one's neighbor does one come to a realization of what it really means to love God. Now that many have lost a capacity for God it is necessary that they become more thoroughly human before they can regain that capability.

To understand what it means to be a believing Christian in the twentieth century, one must first know something about what it has meant to be Christian during the past two thousand years. The previous sections of this study indicate that a general consensus of opinion exists among representative theologians regarding past and present forms of Christian belief, and fidelity demands that new developments be in accordance with earlier determinations. Newman, Rahner and Lonergan all agree on certain fundamental principles regarding the development of religious doctrine within the Church and the traditional interpretation of the Christian doctrine of God. In general, it can be said that there is almost universal agreement among Roman Catholic theologians that Catholic theology is irrevocably committed to certain epistemological presuppositions regarding the nature of truth and divine revelation. According to the theologians treated in this study, the nature of Christian truth is such that it demands an underlying continuity which sets definite limits upon future developments; doctrinal development cannot consist in a completely open-ended process. To some degree, doctrinal evolution must always be continuous and homogeneous; it cannot be radically discontinuous and heterogeneous. Definite boundary conditions have been set upon both the content and the development of religious truth within the Christian community.

Christian truth, although dependent upon certain cultural and historical contingencies, is not wedded to any specific cultural expression. Faith is not bound to a single set of images, even the initial set. It nevertheless expresses something permanent and intelligible; it is addressed to men of all ages and all cultures. Religious dogmas, then, can be viewed as attempts to formulate religious truths in very precise terms, but it must always be remembered that these verbal expressions point beyond themselves to God who is the only absolute reality. This is not to say that religious dogmas are merely symbolic. They are intended to focus attention upon a particular aspect of the divine reality, to convey a sense of mystery, and therefore they should not be viewed as some kind of intellectual word game or logical jigsaw puzzle. They represent unique moments of understanding.

The Christian believer places his faith and confidence in the person of Jesus of Nazareth. Meanwhile, the full meaning of Christian revelation is still being explored, and the Church remains open to new interpretations of the Christian message. Traditional interpretations, however, cannot be overlooked or neglected in this process. Still, modern theologians recognize the need for a new hermeneutic and the need to develop scientific techniques which will assist them in discovering the full meaning of Christian revelation. Fundamental questions regarding the nature of truth and human understanding must be reexamined. Since God's revelation to man is made in spatio-temporal terms, the complexities of language and its relation to human experience must be studied more closely. Christians have a serious obligation to try to uncover the full meaning of God's self-disclosure to man in the person of Christ. This does not mean, however, that the theologians should be viewed as spiritual code-breakers trying to decipher cryptic messages from a remotely distant divine Being. Operating upon the available evidence, within the defined faith-context of the believing community and under the guidance of the Spirit, they work to help the community reach new levels of religious understanding.

While the theologian articulates and explores the faith of the community, the belief of the average Christian is not dependent upon the sophisticated scientific techniques and discoveries of the professional theologian. There is a real difference between faith and theology. The ordinary believer is not expected to suspend his belief until theologians develop a sufficiently refined hermeneutic for interpreting the complete meaning of Christianity. By honestly trying to live his life within the framework of the believing Church and the teachings of Christ, an individual gradually comes to a proper appreciation of what it means to be a Christian.

Because contemporary theology is in a state of fragmentation, it is not surprising that an easy solution to complex problems such as the development of dogma is not forthcoming. The research of men like Dewart, Newman, Rahner and Lonergan, however, has uncovered certain useful principles which serve as helpful guidelines for working toward an adequate theory of doctrinal development.

The Christian community encompasses many philosophies and theologies; there is no exclusively valid approach to the truth of human existence or Christian faith. As a comprehensive interpretation of the world, Christianity must always be forward-looking; it cannot remain content to focus its attention upon the past, important as the past may be. The importance of the eschatological dimension of Christianity is stressed in a new theological movement which has been termed 'the Theology of Hope.' This new thrust of theological speculation, associated with the names of men like Jürgen Moltmann, Wolfhart Pannenberg, Gerhard Sauter and Johannes Metz, draws many of its principal insights from the thought of Ernst Block, a Marxist philosopher.[1] Many commentators feel that this new movement provides answers to the same questions that led to the Death-of-God phenomenon.

These theologians maintain that all Christian teachings are to be defined primarily in terms of eschatology, that is, in terms of the direction in which mankind is moving. Christianity, they claim, *is* eschatology. The Bible and Christ point to a continuing form of revelation in the future; revelation is not to be considered as a once-and-for-all past event. God, they point out, is not a static, a-temporal, reality. He is the one who is coming to man. Having acted in human history in the past, he has also promised to act in the future. The Christian believes that God acts upon history out of the future toward which humanity is moving. To participate in the new world order proclaimed by Christianity, the need for a radical and revolutionary involvement in the world must be recognized. Christianity must develop along the axis which points to the future.

While trying to chart a course between the Scylla of fideism and the Charybdis of rationalism, the committed Christian of today and tomorrow must strive to understand both man and God better, to see revelation and faith as two essential aspects of the interpersonal relation between God and man, to live a life of honesty and integrity and service while remaining open to the Spirit and giving witness to the presence of God in the world in order that others might also come to a clearer recognition of the God in whom we live and move and have our being.

NOTE

1. On the Theology of Hope, see Jürgen Moltmann, *The Theology of Hope* (New York: Harper and Row, 1968).

EDWARD T. WALSH

What Do You Think of Christ?

"WHAT DO YOU THINK of Christ?" is a question that we who are trying to communicate Christianity to others must ask ourselves again and again. We can no longer find the answer ready-made, and we realize that many contradictory answers are being offered. The purpose of this article, then, is to help teachers locate their thinking about Christ in the broad context of Christian thinking through the ages and in our own times, and to suggest some further reading which the author has found helpful.

Jesus of Nazareth was betrayed by Judas who probably felt he was too much a political "dove," arrested by religious leaders who saw him as a heretic, and condemned to death by Roman authority as a rebellious political "hawk." Angry, revolutionary Zealots, Jewish religious leaders, and Roman civil leaders all saw Jesus through the eyes of their own prejudices without really trying to know who he was or what he had to say.

The Zealots had one absolutely consuming passion: Jewish political independence from Rome; the Jewish religious leaders had a neurotic compulsion for

* Father Edward Walsh taught theology at St. Thomas College in St. Paul, Minnesota, and is now studying for a doctorate at the University of Michigan.

legalistic conformity to a set of man-made rules and customs; and the Roman authorities had an ever-present fear of rebellion in Palestine. Each of these groups perceived Jesus as a different kind of threat to their own world and value systems. Instead of allowing the real Jesus to be a catalyst prompting them to re-evaluate their structures, they projected their own unconscious anxieties and doubts upon him. Eventually, he had to pay with his life for failing to conform to existing value systems and thus relieve people of inner doubts about their worth. Dostoevsky's story of the Grand Inquisitor in his *Brothers Karamazov* portrays Church officials as rejecting the real Jesus when he comes to question their way of running his church—everyone is somewhat afraid of truth, love and freedom.

In much the same way, through the centuries and in our own day, theologians and religious educators (parents included) have tried to use Jesus of Nazareth to make their work easier. Thus, he is pictured in art and catechetics as a docile subject, a superman, an anemic altar boy, etc., according to the felt need of the authority or teacher who may be trying to run a "tight ship," explain the man-made concept of "beatific vision" (one wag called it the "big stare" version of heaven) or recruit vocations from the local grammar school. Such distortion is probably more detrimental to the good news of Jesus Christ than his classification as a "criminal" by first century authorities.

What John says about Joe often tells us more about John than it does about Joe. Likewise with much of the Jesus-talk down through the ages. The various understandings and portrayals of this liberating son of Mary often tell us more about the ideals and ideas of perfection prevalent in a particular time and clime than they do about Jesus the Jew.

If anything has become clear from the research and reflection on Jesus of Nazareth during the 20th century, it is that Jesus really was a first-century Jew. Of course, he transcended his culture, but he was nevertheless markedly Jewish. His continued importance to people of every century including our own, however, is due to something more than his genius: he lives as a witness to a life beyond death, a human being alive with God's own life. He was raised by God as an objective echo to the whisper of a hope in the human heart that craves unending and fulfilled existence. Only in the splendor of his unique risen life does his pre-Easter personality draw our attention. The apostle Paul always emphasized the centrality of the resurrection in Christian faith, but the thinking of future centuries lost sight of its importance. (It is significant, however, that through all the developments of the Liturgy from the earliest times to our own, Easter has remained in theory, if not in popular estimation, the most important and central feast in the Christian year.) A brief review of some of the main developments in the understanding of Jesus throughout history should help situate today's vantage point.

From the very beginning of Christianity in small communities around the Mediterranean Sea, different aspects of the richness of the personality of Jesus the Nazarene were emphasized by various writers. Although some fixed tradition of sayings of Jesus seems to have arisen early, great diversity exists among the Christologies of the New Testament. No one understanding of Jesus and his work emerged as *the* orthodox one. One great difference between the variations of Christology in the New Testament and some later and less legitimate ones is that the former give full and primary importance to the risen Jesus while the latter do not.

Even before we come to the great theologians of the New Testament—Paul and John—other New Testament writers used Old Testament categories to present their own Christologies. Jesus was presented as the fulfillment of Jewish hopes. These writers placed their own insights into proper perspective by subordinating their interpretation to the overarching perception that Jesus now rules as Lord over his Church, over the world, and over the life of the Christian. The New Testament views Christ from many angles; in it we have the contrast between a Messianic Christology (speeches in Acts and the Synoptics) and the Johannine idea of the Logos; the leitmotif determining the portrayal of Christ may be salvation history (Synoptics, Romans, Galatians), cosmology (Ephesians and Colossians), liturgy (Hebrews) or prophecy (Revelation).

The second century added to this first-century diversity in understanding and portraying Jesus, becoming the most pluralistic of all centuries in its Christologies. (A bibliography included at the end of this essay indicates possibilities for further reading—this can only be a sketch.) New questions were now being asked about Jesus, and new categories of thought were necessary. The task for the second-century writers (apologists) was to try to explain *how* Jesus was really man and also God. Attention focused on how the divine could unite with the human in Jesus without either being submerged. In some areas, Christians were actually being accused of worshiping a man and, although great variety exists among the second-century apologists, we say generally that most were preoccupied with the question of what we would now call the psychosomatic make-up of Jesus.

A favorite philosophical concept with which these thinkers worked was that of "the Logos," a concept used frequently by the Jewish philosopher-theologian, Philo (died 50 A.D.) to refer to the principal intermediary power between God and man. The understanding of Jesus as the union of Logos and man, as seen in John, had a strong influence in the development of Christology. We might call this a "from above" Christology which emphasized the coming down of the pre-existent Logos and a deification taking place in the incarnation. By contrast, "from below" Christology, which takes its point of departure from the resurrection more than from the incarnation, rises from the historical man, Jesus, to the recognition of his divinity.[1] The Church of the early centuries followed this "from above" approach in forming the Christology which has become "official" through creeds and the early councils.

This emphasis on the Logos was further accentuated when some Alexandrian thinkers (especially Origen, c. 185-254 A.D.) suggested the idea that the Logos was *almost* equal to God. The Council of Nicaea (325 A.D.) said that the Logos was "of the same substance" as the Father, and then the Council of Chalcedon (451 A.D.) capped this development of official Christology by insisting on "two natures" in Jesus, thus excluding any understanding which would have the Logos take the place of Jesus' human soul.

This Chalcedonian definition marked the end of official statements from the Church about Jesus. Theological currents became popular, emphasizing this or that aspect of Jesus' person or work, but there have been no official shifts of emphasis in Christology since the crystallization of the "from above" approach in the 5th century at Chalcedon.

In the 11th and 12th centuries, the penitential practice of the medieval church determined the viewpoint of its Christology. Sin was seen as an infinite offense against God which could be compensated for only by satisfaction equally infinite—Anselm of Canterbury's *Cur Deus Homo?* (1094-98) portrayed Jesus as paying a debt to God.

Although there were impulses in the direction of a Christology which started with the man Jesus (*i.e.*, "from below") in the Middle Ages, the major efforts were directed towards a systematization and elaboration of the Nicaean and Chalcedonian pronouncements of the ancient Church. Martin Luther, after his epoch-making break with the medieval Church, emphasized the "office" of Jesus as the man who bore God's wrath for us.

One major turning point in reflection about Jesus came with the Enlightenment in the 18th century. Here the inquiry did center around the man, Jesus, but not in the context of his unity with God in the full sense of earlier Christological dogma. In this rationalistic approach, the historical perspective became central, and traditional dogma meant little. New questions were posed about Jesus, and the transition from gospel to Church creeds was examined with the critical eye of historical scholarship. Suspicion was aroused that Jesus of Nazareth was possibly the most misunderstood personality of all time.

New "Lives of Christ" were written, supposedly improving upon the dogmatic coldness of the creeds. Each author projected his own idealism upon Jesus with little concern for a critical understanding of what the

New Testament really said about him. Friedrich Schleiermacher (1768-1834) emphasized Jesus' consciousness and feeling for the presence of God—ignoring any emphasis on "salvation" beyond that which comes with a consciousness of God's presence in this life. Emmanuel Kant (1724-1804) and Albrecht Ritschl (1822-1889) differed somewhat from Schleiermacher in emphasizing Jesus as an ethical example for all men. It is easy to perceive in the background, especially of Ritschl's portrayal of Jesus, the ideals of the 19th century. "Jesus" was just a name these men gave to their own projections of the ideal man.

The death knell was sounded over such attempts to portray the historical Jesus by Martin Kahler's essay, "The So-Called Historical Jesus and the Biblical Christ of Faith" (1892). Kahler showed that the Jesus of the 19th century biographers was not the Jesus of the New Testament. Albert Schweitzer's *Quest of the Historical Jesus* put the finishing touches on the grave of this kind of quest for the historical Jesus by showing that the Nazarene was a first-century Jew in the fullest sense of that word—not a 19th or 20th century altruist.

Schweitzer's publication, especially, returned Jesus to his own time and place in history. Jesus' emphasis on God's intervention which alone could bring history to fulfillment, Schweitzer said, is basically incompatible with modern notions of religion and morality. Attempts to contemporize Jesus by deleting eschatology from his outlook collapse under the scrutiny of historical research. Schweitzer himself was no more comfortable with the Jesus he had insisted upon than anyone else—he never dreamed he would live to see eschatology become the heart of theology!

Skepticism set in as scholars were forced to abandon the original quest for the historical Jesus. It was gradually acknowledged that the gospels are not primarily sources for the life of the pre-Easter Jesus, but rather testimonies to his followers' belief in him as the Christ ("anointed one" of God). This shift in perspective brought about a new approach as the dialectical theologians (Karl Barth, Emil Brunner, Friedrich Gogarten, Rudolph Bultmann and Paul Tillich) disclaimed the historical Jesus and justified their neglect of history by quoting the apostle Paul's second letter to the Corinthians: "Though we have known Christ after the flesh, yet now we know him thus no more" (5:16). In their efforts to free Christology from its dependence on historical studies which sometime threatened to subordinate faith to historical inquiry, but following Kahler in placing their confidence in the living word and the testimony of the Holy Spirit, these thinkers divorced Christology from the historical Jesus.

However understandable this emphasis on faith rather than historical scholarship may have been in the context of the times, a Christ apart from the historical Jesus is just a pious concoction. It is not equating historical inquiry with faith to say that we can never be unconcerned with the historical man, Jesus. Concrete historical facts are all we have to distinguish intelligently placed faith from emotional credulity. Going beyond historical facts in faith is not the same as ignoring history entirely.

Rudolph Bultmann was the main figure in this emphasis on the preached Christ rather than the historical Jesus. He seemed to regard concern with historical origins as a sign of a lack of faith, but there

was some ambiguity in his position; *e.g.,* he *did* emphasize the bare fact of Jesus' historicity and his death on
the cross.

The disciples of Bultmann, called post-Bultman-
nians, have inaugurated what has come to be called
"the new quest for the historical Jesus." These men
have learned their lessons well from their teacher but
are convinced that more can be known about the
Nazarene underlying the kerygma than Bultmann realized. The year 1954 marks the date of the first
publication in the new quest: "The Problem of the Historical Jesus," by Ernst Kasemann. Following Kasemann's essay, which suggested that more can be known
about Jesus than simply that he lived and died, Gunther
Bornkamm, in 1956, published his monograph, *Jesus
of Nazareth,* which has quite a good deal to say about
the historical Jesus.

This brief sketch of some of the main developments in Christology brings us up to our present time
where the relation between Jesus and the kerygma has
become the crucial question in current New Testament
study. Before turning our attention to the problem of
the resurrection and its historicity, we might summarize
what even critically-minded New Testament exegetes
will agree upon today regarding the historical Jesus:

He was a first-century Jew who lived and thought in
the world of first-century Judaism in Palestine. He died
a violent death on the cross because of some special
claims he made. He is a very marked type of individual
who cannot be fictional according to the law of probability. His preaching was characteristically composed of
short, pregnant sentences which fixed themselves easily
in the memory. Exegetes and historians also agree that
the inadequate blending of sayings of Jesus in the

Synoptic gospels indicates that the evangelists were probably tied to a tradition of sayings which they did not feel free to ignore or adjust very much, even when these sayings made their own narrative awkward.

In the developments discussed so far, with the exception of the New Testament, little or no emphasis has been put on the resurrection as an historical event in the life of Jesus or the early Church. Yet it is his resurrection which makes Jesus unique among great charismatic religious leaders in human history (in the sense that teachings similar to those of Jesus, such as the Golden Rule, are to be found in other religious literature).

During the 1950's, especially, there were a number of full-scale studies of the resurrection.[2] More recently, two young German theologians have published major works with the resurrection as the cornerstone of their Christology, Jürgen Moltmann and Wolfhart Pannenberg, whose works are in diametrical opposition to the devaluation of Easter as an historical event in modern liberal theology.

Because Easter is a unique event in human history which cannot be compared with any similar experience of mankind, we do not have adequate concepts and words with which to discuss it. But there would be no gospel, not one account, no letter in the New Testament, no faith, no Church, no worship, no prayer in Christian communities to this day without the message of the resurrection of Jesus.

The undeniable tension between the singleness of the Easter *message* and the ambiguity and historical problems of the various Easter *narratives* has prompted some liberal theologians to consider the event as theologically true but historically non-existent.

Difficulties in gaining a satisfactory idea of how the Easter events occurred may be classified as historical, anthropological, and psychological. As to the historical, anyone who compares the conflicting gospel resurrection stories will recognize the variety of chronological sequence and geographical location of Jesus' appearances. As to the anthropological, there is the distinction between what was experienced and its articulation in imagery taken from the current notions about man's composition (*i.e.,* Hebrews conceived of man as an animated body while Greeks conceived of him as an incarnated spirit). As to the psychological, there is the question of the reliability of the witnesses and the validity of their alleged experiences. (Each of these areas is addressed in publications listed in the bibliography. I will pass over them here and borrow heavily from Pannenberg in sketching a modern approach to the resurrection.)

In a biblical perspective, the essences of things are decided by what they finally become. In such a dynamic viewpoint, Jesus' resurrection would be emphasized rather than his incarnation. It has become more and more common among biblical scholars to admit that Jesus was probably ignorant of many things, just like any other man.[3] Quite possibly, this ignorance extended not only to questions such as when history would end, but also to his own person. To hold to the probability of some psychological development in Jesus' self-knowledge does not deny that he was always one with God in a unique manner, but only that it took time, suffering and even death to bring him to full awareness of who he was—as is the case with every man. One author puts it thus: "Jesus was what he is before he knew about it."

What Jesus seems to have expected for all of history in his own time took place instead in himself alone at Easter—he became a living symbol of the End of Time ahead of time, an anticipation of God's final victory over sin and death in every man, or, as Pannenberg puts it: "the prolepsis of the eschaton." It has become fashionable in some allegedly Christian circles to de-emphasize life beyond death. What may have started as a healthy and Christian corrective for a quietistic piety which did not take this earthly life seriously enough has become—even in some Roman Catholic writers and speakers—a practical denial of anything except earthly existence. Jesus is presented quite rightly as "the Man for others," but his intense expectation of future fulfillment beyond death and history is seen as naïve and childish. *It is important to emphasize that if this apocalyptic expectation goes, so does authentic Christian faith.* And such expectation is not as naïve and unsophisticated as some pseudo-intellectuals would have us believe. These words of Pannenberg should be pondered:

One may presumably characterize it as a generally demonstrable anthropological finding that the definition of the essence of man does not come to ultimate fulfillment in the finitude of his earthly life. Only if the individual man has his destiny exclusively in the community of humanity, if he thus finds the purpose of his existence completely absorbed as an individual in humanity as it is at hand in his concrete society, only then would the idea of a life beyond death be something to be relinquished. . . .

Thus, the best modern thinking encourages us to study and to present Jesus in a "from below" perspective, complementing the "from above" perspective dominant in the past, as very much a real man of first-century Judaism, but also a man who transcends time with his consciousness of the intimacy and power of God, and of God's love for all men. Jesus was a man of his own time, but he is the Man for our time as, through his teaching and example, he shows us how we must love one another since God has first loved us, excluding any provincialism in our love and concern. He is the Man for our times since, without being an anarchist, he did not hesitate to violate man-made laws and customs when these dictated something less than love for every man.

But he is also the Man for our times in his unshakable confidence in his Father's power to bring him through death to a new and unimaginable fullness of life and in the vindication of that confidence through his resurrection. The living, risen Christ is the Man for our times as God's witness that every person is eternally precious, and that failure, disease, and death are not the ultimate realities, that life and love will finally prevail. True Christian discipleship, then, means living life with the boldness, honesty, and freedom that love demands, and doing so in the strength of our hope, already realized in Christ, that truth and love will ultimately reign over all reality and that we will share in this victory.

RECOMMENDED READING

For a history of reflection on Jesus:

1) Early centuries in detail
   Aloys Grillmeier, *Christ in Christian Tradition*
   (Sheed & Ward, N.Y., 1965)

> J. N. D. Kelly, *Early Christian Doctrines* (Adam and Charles Black, London, 1960)

2) Quests for the historical Jesus

> James M. Robinson, *A New Quest for the Historical Jesus* (SCM Press, London, 1959)

> Commonweal's *Jesus Papers,* Nov. 24, 1967, especially articles by Avery Dulles and Raymond Brown.

> Raymond Brown, *Jesus—God and Man* (Bruce, Milwaukee, 1967)

> Carl E. Braaten, *History and Hermeneutics* (Westminster, Philadelphia, 1966)

3) Classic work of synthesis (historical, philosophical, theological)

> Wolfhart Pannenberg, *Jesus: God and Man* (Westminster, Philadelphia, 1968)

4) A "Life of Christ" to replace those outdated by contemporary scholarship

> Gunther Bornkamm, *Jesus of Nazareth* (Harper and Row, N.Y., 1960)

NOTES

1. See Pannenberg's book in bibliography, pp. 33ff.

2. Durwell's *The Resurrection,* published in English in 1960 (Sheed & Ward, N.Y.), marked a major shift in Catholic thinking.

3. Raymond Brown's small book listed in the bibliography.

WILLIAM H. SHANNON

Christian Conscience

IN *The Difficulties of Anglicans,* John Henry New-man concludes his section on conscience with an oft-quoted passage: "If I am obliged to bring religion into after-dinner toasts (which indeed does not seem quite the thing) I shall drink—to the Pope, if you please,—but still to Conscience first and to the Pope after-wards."

I begin with this quotation from Newman because it emphasizes what has always been an essential element of Catholic moral teaching, though sometimes a forgotten one—namely, the unique role in our moral life of personal conscience. In our moral teaching today, it seems to me, we must face among other things, three especially urgent questions—questions which we must answer more adequately than we have in the past. The first two are theoretical questions: What precisely is conscience? What do we mean by the primacy of conscience in our moral life? The third question is an eminently practical one: How do we help people to develop a mature personal conscience?

Before attempting the first question and discussing what conscience is, I should like to speak briefly about two prevalent attitudes toward conscience—both of which I think are inadequate and even erroneous.

* Monsignor William Shannon is on the Liturgical Commission of the diocese of Rochester, New York. This is the text of a talk he delivered to the Sisters of St. Joseph, Rochester.

The first attitude I refer to is the tendency to exteriorize conscience and thus to depersonalize it. In this view conscience for all practical purposes is equated with the external law. The judgment as to whether an act is good or bad is made simply by juxtaposing the action I have performed and the external law, with little personal decision being involved. Frequently this juxtaposing of my action and the external law takes place only post factum. In such a view of conscience sin becomes, not so much the personal decision of saying "no" to God, but rather something that happens to me. This way of conceiving conscience often comes to light in the confessional. A person enters the confessional and in effect says to the priest: "I have done such and such. Have I committed a sin?" On one side of the confessional screen is the penitent who presents his action for evaluation; on the other side is the priest who presumably has the knowledge of the law. Confession consists of bringing these two together, namely the action and the law, so that a judgment may be made. If the priest says: "No. That was not a sin," the penitent breathes a sigh of relief. He has been acquitted. There was no sin after all. If the priest's answer is: "Yes," then the penitent's reaction may well be: "I was afraid it was. Now that I know I have committed sin, I am sorry. Please give me absolution."

This mentality which tends to turn conscience from being a personal judgment that a man makes on his own actions into a judgment that is made for him, is the unhappy and unhealthy situation produced all too often by the kind of moral indoctrination we have given in the past. We have tried in our moral teaching (whether in the classroom, the pulpit or the confessional) to be the consciences of others, to dictate their judgment of conscience. Being the conscience of another may seem to be an easier task than helping them to develop mature consciences of their own. But for such tactics we pay a frightful price. This exteriorizing of conscience does great harm to the Christian community. It keeps people perpetually adolescent in their moral response. It effectively stifles any moral initiative on their part.

But there is a second attitude toward conscience which is almost the reverse of the first and which equally, though not so evidently, thwarts genuine moral growth. This I would call the over-interiorization of conscience. If the first attitude so exteriorizes conscience as to depersonalize moral judgment, the second attitude represents a tendency to interiorize conscience in such a way as to isolate it from anything exterior to the person that should enter into the decision of conscience. The decision of conscience is isolated from the concrete historical situation of the person who makes the decision. It is isolated too from the demands of the Gospel and from the corporate wisdom and experience of the Christian community.

Such a mentality makes the individual conscience the unique source of moral values rather than the personal discovery and experience of moral values. The individual approaches each moral decision armed only with the personal insights that are his own, ignoring the insights of others, even of the Christian community or even scorning those insights as a threat to personal decision-making.

If the first attitude is the result of a false moral indoctrination that distrusts personal decision, the second results from the present moral confusion which equates freedom of conscience with a personal moral autonomy that refuses to look beyond the self for moral values. The first attitude leads to moral rigidity; the second leads to moral chaos. At first sight the second attitude toward conscience might appear to be the more mature; at closer examination it is seen in fact to be simply a different species of immaturity.

In the moral teaching that we engage in we must face the fact that increasingly with the young we are going to meet with the second attitude rather than the first. Our great temptation is apt to be that we shall be so concerned about the chaos generated by this mentality that we shall want to return to the former approach of dictating the decision of conscience as being at least the safer course of action. We must resist this temptation, with the realization that we cannot turn the clock back and with the conviction that the moral rigidity of the first attitude toward conscience is as reprehensible as the moral irresponsibility of the second. Our energies must be directed toward the formation of a right attitude toward conscience.

Our problem, then, is to develop an understanding of conscience that avoids both these extremes. Conscience is not simply a dictate which comes from without, neither is it an autonomous creator of moral values that operates solely within the individual.

In attempting to clarify the meaning of conscience I do not intend to begin with a definition of conscience. I am not sure that conscience can be defined in such a way that the definition will tell us precisely what it is. Definitions are, of course, useful tools. But we must be careful to use them only as tools. There is so much more to a reality than can be gotten into a definition. The reality of conscience is too complex a notion to be circumscribed by the terms of a simple definition. I prefer rather to begin with a description of conscience.

The reality of conscience is the experience of responsibility. We all understand this. Conscience tells me that my action is mine and that I am accountable for it. But conscience not only tells me I am responsible for the separate moral actions I perform. It also tells me that I am responsible, within certain limits at least, for the moral being that I build up gradually through the actions I perform. Conscience, therefore, is the experience of responsibility not only for what I do but for what I am. The context in which this responsibility is experienced is the exercise of freedom. We are aware that we are accountable for our actions, only if they are truly our own; and they are truly our own only if they are free.

Conscience, therefore, may be described as the experience of responsibility in the exercise of freedom. If our understanding of conscience, then, is to be made precise, we must clarify the meaning of freedom and the meaning of responsibility. This is what I propose to do now.

By freedom I mean the power of self-determination which sets man apart from all other beings. Man does not "exist," like a plant or animal, harnessed to a natural order which totally determines his nature. A plant or an animal becomes what it is by internal necessity, by a determination fixed in nature. Man on the other hand becomes what he becomes by self-determination. He has, within limits of course, the capability of determining for himself what he will become. In other words, man "exists" in a situation of openness. He is open to various possibilities of self-realization. His most important task in life is to discover who he is and become who he is. And he becomes who he is not by some internal compulsion over which he has no control, but by choosing the self he will be. It is in this sense that we can say with the existentialists that man's existence precedes his essence. His freedom is a summons to become himself, to realize through his own choices the historical possibilities of his selfhood.

This is the positive aspect of human freedom—this freedom in view of something, this freedom *for* something—the freedom to objectivize the capabilities of his being, to realize himself as a person, to become as fully a man as he can.

This freedom of self-realization, as I have described it, expresses an ideal or, if you will, an abstraction. For man's power of self-determination does not exist in a vacuum, but is historically situated. By that I mean that man strives to become himself in a concrete set of historical circumstances and in inter-relations with other persons. These historical circumstances may help or impede his personal growth. The persons he meets with may open or close themselves to him and thus limit or expand the scope of his freedom and its exercise.

There is then in man this constant tension between his drive for self-realization and the actual historical situation in which he finds himself and which influences the way in which this drive is actually realized. Take the example of a boy who is brought up in an environment where slashing automobile tires, breaking into stores and taking dope are normal forms of recreation. In the case of such a boy we may well question whether he is to be blamed for his transgressions. We may say that the guilt falls not on him but on those who see the situation which victimizes him and allow it to continue to exist. But whether he is held guilty or not, his capability of achieving authentic self-realization is seriously hampered by the historical situation in which, through no choice of his own, he finds himself.

In other words, a man comes into this world at a particular time, in a particular place and in a given community of men and women. He has the internal freedom to become himself, but the historical condition into which he is born may wonderfully expand or severely limit the objectivization of that freedom. If he is to become as fully a man as he can, it is not enough that he be free *for* self-realization; he must also be free *from* intolerable and inhuman conditions that prevent the achievement of authentic selfhood.

Having discussed what freedom is and how its actual realization is affected by the situation in which it is exercised, I should like to move one point further and discuss the question: How does this freedom of man to achieve authentic self-hood express itself?

The answer may be stated very simply: it expresses itself in two ways: in man's actions and in his basic options or radical choices. It is in this light that we can distinguish freedom of action and freedom of option. This distinction is an important one; yet much of our moral training has ignored the second and consequently overemphasized the first (almost as if it were the unique expression of human freedom). Now there is no doubt that the most evidently recognizable expression of freedom is the freedom that we recognize in our actions. A man is free to act or not to act. He is free to act in one way or another. He is free to choose this object or that.

But what we need to realize more fully is that

freedom involves not only what I do but what I am and what I want to become. It is not enough to see freedom embodied in isolated individual acts. Freedom at its deepest level is expressed in the radical choice that I make of the basic direction that I want my life to take. This is what I mean by freedom of option. Karl Rahner calls it "freedom of being." It is the positioning of my freedom toward a particular direction. It is the orientating of my freedom toward authentic self-realization or its opposite.

In other words, underlying a man's day-to-day decisions is an enduring choice that determines the basic thrust of his life. This basic option exercises a directive influence on the other choices he makes, on the actions he performs. Human actions, therefore, are, to a greater or lesser degree, an expression of man's basic option. Some actions are so momentous in their very substance that it is difficult to think of them as not embodying the fundamental orientation of a man's life; other actions, on the contrary, appear so unimportant or peripheral in their materiality that it is scarcely possible to think of them as embodying this basic option. When a negative basic option clearly manifests itself in human actions, we speak of mortal sin. Venial sin, on the other hand, is an action which involves a bad choice, but one that is so superficial or unfree that it simply cannot be said to embody the basic option of life.

If I may put this in another way: the basic option of a Christian in grace is a choice explicitly for God. His basic moral stance is to say yes to God. When he does not act consistently with that basic choice, he commits venial sin. But that basic choice remains till he changes it by mortal sin. For this is precisely what

mortal sin is: a reversal of that fundamental choice
that governs his life. It is the adoption of a new moral
stance: it is saying "no" to God.

This distinction between freedom of action and
freedom of option is of far-reaching and practical
importance in our own moral life and in our teaching
of morality.

It helps us to understand that the Christian moral
life must be viewed, not as a static unchanging response
in isolated actions to certain moral demands, but
rather as an ever-deepening growth in our lives of the
influence of the radical choice to which Christian bap-
tism commits us. More and more our life and its individual actions need to be brought under the influence
of this radical choice.

Such an understanding of true moral growth would
make our approach to the sacrament of penance more
meaningful. It would help us to see that in this moment
of encounter with the healing Christ we should be
concerned, not simply with our failures in particular
actions, but rather with the basic direction in which
our lives are moving. Do our individual actions indicate
a basic growth in unselfishness or in its opposite?

We need also to stress this distinction in helping
young people to form sound and mature consciences.
For example, when a young man and a young woman
encounter difficulties in matters of chastity, we need to
help them concentrate their attention not so much
on the failures they may experience in individual actions, but on the basic direction in which their relationship is moving. Are they genuinely striving to make
their love for one another more truly unselfish? Are
they sincerely striving, even though not always suc-
ceeding, to think not simply of the enjoyment of the

moment, but of what is truly and ultimately best for both of them? Or, on the other hand, have they reached a point where anything goes, where their relationship involves a great deal of self-seeking and mutual exploitation of one another? In other words, we have to help them see their individual actions, not in isolation, but as the embodiment of a basic direction in which their loving is moving.

At this point it will help to recall the description of conscience with which we began—that conscience is the experience of responsibility in the exercise of freedom. We have discussed the meaning of freedom. We have seen that it is the power of self-realization that operates within a given set of historical circumstances and expresses itself in man's actions and in his radical choices. It is time now to clarify what we mean by the experience of responsibility.

We readily recognize a correlation between freedom and responsibility. We disclaim responsibility for any of our actions that are not free. We admit our responsibility for what we do freely. We expect to be held accountable for our free actions.

Yet it should be noted that there is a certain ambiguity about the word "responsibility." It may be used in a passive sense, meaning that others hold me responsible for what I do; or it may be used in an active sense, meaning that I am truly acting responsibly in a given situation. For to say that I am held responsible for what I do does not necessarily mean that what I have done is a truly responsible action. At times, in fact, I may be held responsible for behavior that is irresponsible. The fact that I am responsible for my actions does not necessarily make me a responsible person. The fact that I am held accountable for my actions does not necessarily mean that I can give a rational account of my actions. Being responsible for an action means more than being taken to task for having done it after I act; it also means taking sufficient thought about it before I act.

In other words responsibility in the active sense of the word includes the notion of responsiveness. In any given situation, I must respond to the moral demands that I am able to discover in that situation. This means a number of things. It means that I must respond to the moral richness that is revealed to me in the very uniqueness of this situation. It means that I must respond to the Law of Christ and to the law of my nature, especially in the light of the insights offered to me by the tested wisdom and experience of the Christian community. It means that I must respond to the inspirations of the indwelling Spirit of God who reveals to me in the depth of my consciousness the demands of the law of love in the concrete situation that I confront.

This responsiveness to the inspirations of the indwelling Spirit is a dimension of Christian conscience that we have too long neglected. We have perhaps been so concerned to make conscience a purely rational act —a judgment of practical reason, St. Thomas calls it— that we have forgotten the words of Jesus: "But when your Advocate has come, whom I will send you from the Father—he will bear witness to me." (John 15:26) "When he comes who is the Spirit of truth, he will guide you into all the truth." (John 16:13) It seems to me that the Council Fathers are speaking of this dimension of conscience when they tell us (*Pastoral Constitution on the Church in the Modern World,* art. 16): "Conscience is the most secret core and sanctuary of a man. There he is alone with God, whose voice echoes in his depths. In a wonderful manner conscience reveals that law which is fulfilled by love of God and neighbor."

But, once I have brought to bear on the situation all the lights that I can discover I must make my own decision. No one else, whether priest, bishop or Pope, can make it for me. This is what we mean when we speak of the primacy of conscience in our moral life. External laws and human authority are indispensable helps for me in arriving at the decision of conscience; but they can never be my conscience. They can never substitute for my conscience. The decision of conscience must be my own. It is a decision in which a man faces his God—alone. The decision he makes is as personal as the divine call which it answers. It is a decision into which a man puts his whole being, weighing his own authenticity in the balance.

The final question I want to discuss is: How do we help people, especially the young, to develop mature Christian consciences? This, of course, is the heart of the problem we face when teaching moral doctrine. There are no simple answers to the question. I shall be content to suggest a few guidelines.

1. We must communicate moral doctrine to our students; at the same time we must encourage them to think for themselves. The two must go hand in hand. Only if they are given a knowledge of moral truth can their thinking for themselves be truly responsible; only if they are thinking for themselves will the moral doctrine we communicate to them become convictions personally held by them.

For there is a great deal of difference between convictions personally held by me and unassimilated knowledge that I have received into my mind but never made my own.

Much of the moral knowledge—indeed the faith-knowledge also—of Catholics belongs to the second category rather than the first. Impersonal sets of propositions—inadequately understood and never reflected upon—have been stored up in their minds. They know these propositions. They can recite them accurately on request. But they have never really appropriated them by personal assent. They have never made them their own intellectually and psychologically.

We cannot be content merely to communicate moral information. We have to confront our students with this information and help them to make it genuinely their own. We have to help them to be honest with themselves and dare to face at some time in their lives what can be a very upsetting question, namely the question: How much of what I have been taught do I really believe and how much do I simply preserve as closed formulas without ever really examining them? We have to be prudent, of course, in bringing about this confrontation. We are not asking them to examine what they believe with a view to rejecting it but rather with a view to assimilating it, appropriating it, making it their own. Until they do this, these truths are not really going to be vital influences in their lives (especially in their adult lives). They may go through the external motions of acting on them, either from routine or worse still from fear; but their hearts will not be in it. And oftentimes a crisis in their lives, that they break under, will reveal how superficial their moral commitment really was.

We have to be on our guard against a subtle unconscious dishonesty on our own part. All too readily we tend to put a premium on submissiveness. We are happy with those who give external agreement to what we teach them. We may be inclined to be suspicious of those who show a tendency to think for themselves—especially when their thinking does not always come out the same way as ours. Yet we need to have faith in them—faith that, if we help them gradually to make their thinking truly responsible, they may end up much better off than the ones who refused to think and were quite content to "swallow" everything we told them.

2. We must help them to see the corporate dimensions of Christian moral doctrine. Christian moral doctrine must not be looked upon simply as impersonal laws handed down by authority—laws that we must simply submit to. Rather, increasingly, we must come to view moral doctrine as the tested wisdom and experience of the whole Christian community. This is not to deny a place of unique importance to the authority of the Church in teaching moral doctrine. It is simply to say that the teaching authority of the Church operates at its best when it listens to the Spirit speaking in the whole Church. The Council Fathers in the *Constitution on the Church* speak of the faithful as a whole bearing witness to the truth of the Gospel: "The body of the faithful as a whole, anointed as they are by the Holy One, cannot err in matters of belief." (art. 12) After all, there is so little in the way of explicitly revealed moral doctrine in the Scriptures. Moreover, moral issues oftentimes can be so very complex. It makes sense, then, that Christian morality should be clarified through the very living of the Christian life. It makes sense that the whole Christian community, in whom the Spirit operates, should be involved, under the direction of the hierarchy, in clarifying the response that Christians should make to the demands of

the Gospel. The task of the teaching Church, then, is not to stifle the Spirit, but rather, in the words of John's first epistle (1 John 4:1) to test the Spirit, to see that it is of God.

3. We must strive to communicate to our students a sense of joy in the living of the Christian life. They must not see their moral life "as the price they have to pay to save their souls," but rather as a joyful response to God our Father who loves us and who creates in us the capability of loving Him in return.

Our moral life, in other words, must be seen as built around grace, not around sin. We must replace a sin-mentality with a grace-mentality. We must make it clear that a Christian is one whose ordinary life is the life of grace, not a constant moving to and fro, from grace to sin, from sin to grace.

This means that our students must be made to understand more fully the radical choice for God which is the essence of the Christian life and the fact that mortal sin involves a reversal of that radical choice. We must never let them confuse mortal sin with something that is completely different from it, namely venial sin. Mortal sin and venial sin are not two species of the genus "sin." The difference between them is not just a matter of degree. They differ in kind one from another. For venial sin means acting inconsistently with the radical option of our lives—something we all do at times; mortal sin is a deliberate reversal of that option.

In conclusion I would simply say that we must respect the inviolable dignity of personal conscience. With Newman we may well drink a toast to conscience, that "most secret core and sanctuary of a man," where he is alone with God.

FERGUS KERR, O.P.

Eschatology as Politics

CHRISTIANITY IS NOTHING IF it is not eschatology:
a hope in a promise for the future. This is what Jürgen
Moltmann is inviting us to take seriously, in his very
important book.[1] It is, however, a difficult book, at
least for the non-theologian; and perhaps the best way
of giving a fair account of its value is to present, in
some detail, the argument of the concluding chapter
(the appendix on Ernst Bloch has been omitted from
the English edition). The problem is to show how
Christianity as eschatology actually *happens*. What
visible form and observable shape does this hope in a
promised future, which believers share, actually take
in the complicated business which is modern life in an
industrial society such as ours? What in fact is the
relationship between the Church and the world?

We have to decide whether, as believers in modern society, we form what Moltmann calls an accom-
modating group, a group capable of being absorbed
and assimilated by society, or a group which is inas-
similable and non-conformist. We have to ask if this
hope in the future which we have, compels us to resist
being assimilated and adjusted to modern society.
Moltmann is, of course, going to argue that if believers
really conduct their lives and their thinking in the

* Father Fergus Kerr is a distinguished English theologian, lecturer and writer.

context of their hope in God's promised future, then there will always be tension between the believing community and modern society . . . whatever modern society may happen to be (Moltmann clearly works in terms of the society to which he belongs: western industrial capitalism).

Moltmann accepts Hegel's analysis of what is characteristic and defining about modern industrial society. Some of the typically Hegelian concepts are muffled by periphrastic constructions in the English translation: I shall highlight them in my summary of Moltmann's argument. His principal source is Hegel's *Philosophy of Law* (1820).

Believers have to do with the society they are in, if they have to do with any society at all, which is the question. In our society it has seemed evident, at least since Hegel's time, that the whole network of relationships created and sustained by the industrial-commercial system of labour extends far into our social-political life and deeply affects our private-domestic life. Following Hegel, as Marx did too on this issue, Moltmann takes it for granted that in an industrial-commercial society such as ours it is the relationships established among us by our work, the interdependencies created by the conditions, demands and goals of our labour, which shape and structure the rest of our relationships: our political relationships (our political system has to do either with preserving or with changing our industrial system) and our domestic relationships (home life is dominated by working life, either because we use the privacy of family life as an escape from the drudgery of work or because the drudgery of work makes it impossible for us to use our leisure creatively at all). Neither our social-political nor our private-domestic relationships lose their substantial autonomy, but they are under constant pressure to do so. Commerce, the exchange of things between one man and another, the exchange of commodities of one sort and another, tends to affect all our relationships: one has only to think of how metaphors from business deals and commercial transactions spread into the language of politics and of personal relationships.

This is what Moltmann calls the reduction of all human relationships to terms of things, *die Verdinglichung aller Beziehungen*. We allow all human relationships to be affected, if not created and defined, by commercial transactions, by the exchange of commodities, by market values. You begin to wonder what you can get out of other people, you begin to treat people as things, and so on.

What is defining about our society, then, is that in contradistinction to all previous societies, human relationships are determined and structured primarily in terms of the conditions, demands and goals of the industrial-commercial system. Everything else (this is the crucial point) is excluded from the category of what is essential for human relationships. We are related to one another as producers and consumers, we are related by the roles which we play in the industrial-commercial system; but we need not be related to one another in any other way whatever. It is no longer important, for instance, that we should live in our own tribe; it is no longer important that we should all worship together. We just have to do our jobs, and for the rest we are *free*. If it is true that the only necessary social bonds we have with one another are basically and definingly the industrial-commercial relationships which we have with one another, then we are *liberated* from one another in new ways, as well as in danger of thinking and feeling only in terms of the exchange of things. For, as Hegel himself pointed out, what so many of those who go on about the horrors of modern society often forget, is that the time in which we are newly tempted to treat people as things is also the time in which we are newly enabled to treat people as persons, as individuals. *Verdinglichung* goes with *Individualität*. The society in which the only necessary bonds which unite people are the industrial-commercial ones, threatening as they do to destroy all our other relationships, is also the society in which people are freer than ever before to enter into relationships. Marriage for love, friendship, trade unions . . . there is a whole spectrum of phenomena which indicate the freedom we have now as individuals, precisely because the old tribal, religious and suchlike bonds have vanished. You don't, for instance, have to worship in our society; you have only to work, and this is what makes it so different from any previous form of society.

All the other relationships we have, except the relationships created by our work, have ceased to be socially necessary and become optional. We must *choose* to worship. The mass-society created by the modern industrial-commercial system is also, in principle, a society in which the individual can be freer, and can thus be more of a person, than in any previous form of society. We can experience ourselves as subjects, precisely because the society of *Verdinglichung* is also the society of *Individualität,* in Hegel's terminology. Organization man can, in principle, be more of an individual than any form of man who has ever lived. Conformity and individualism have their roots in the same datum: in the fact that the only essential, socially necessary relations which we have now are our industrial-commercial ones. Destroying as it has done the whole tribal-feudal-sacral society that went before it, modern society has, in principle and to some extent even in practice, made it possible for us to be more choosing, more individual, than was ever possible before.

The task is, of course, to maintain the tension between mass-organization of the industrial-commercial system (*Vermassung*) and the development of personal choice in relationships (*Subjektivität*), so that we may become more and more individuals without lapsing out into eccentricity and eventually into privacy and solipsism.

Moltmann can now ask what has happened to the Church during this period in which society has developed into a mass-society carrying with it the possibility of more privacy than ever before. In the pre-industrial era the Church continued to play the role which it had been given by the Emperor Constantine in the middle of the fourth century: Christianity was in fact the state religion, the *cultus publicus,* the sacralization of the status quo.[2] Religion was socially necessary. Everybody was a believer. Every member of society was at the same time a member of the Church, unless he publicly opted out, which was often a dangerous course to take. You worshipped with the same social pressure and necessity to do so as you worked. But in the new industrial society, from the late eighteenth century onwards, you no longer had to worship . . . all you had to do was to work. There is no denying how destructive this was for millions of people: what happened to the English peasants and rural labourers, uprooted from the feudal-sacral society with its securities, including compulsory religion, is a matter of history. The destruction of social bonds exposed several generations to unprecedented exploitation and brutality, though in the long run it was to make a new freedom possible.

Christianity ceased to be the established religion. It ceased to be so at least in principle and in effect, though it has gone on, in this country at least, entirely and ceremonially oblivious to this until our own time. Instead of being the *cultus publicus*, Christianity became a *cultus privatus*. Going to church, worshipping God, seeking the absolute, has ceased to be a public obligation and a social duty, and become an optional, voluntary, private activity. A man's religion is now his own affair.

This opens the way to one form of Christianity which Moltmann attacks with vigour: Christianity as the cult appropriate to the new individualism possible within mass industrial society. Here, it is clear, he is attacking the influence of the theology of Rudolf Bultmann. Out of the German Lutheran tradition itself, that is to say, he is making the kind of criticism which Brian Wicker has made on various occasions.[3] We could practise some self-criticism as Catholics on this score too.

This is the kind of theology which accepts the division between man as trapped in industrial-commercial relationships and man as a private person, and goes on to abandon the whole social-political side of human life to concentrate on saving man as a private person. The situations in which Christian faith is regarded as operative are our 'encounters', so long as they have nothing to do with the structures of the social-economic system in which we live. Faith is regarded as so 'transcendental' that it occurs outside the context of any meanings and purposes which are socially and politically communicable and verifiable. It is consistent with this that Christian experience cannot be shaped by institutions of any kind. Christian love is something that happens in the pure spontaneity of intimate I-and-thou situations; but the whole social-political dimension of human life, not to speak of the industrial-commercial system, is reduced to mere organization, devoid of any human meaning. Politics is merely a matter of keeping the streets clean. Your neighbour is the man you meet in personal encounter, not the man with whom you are involved in any social-political situation. The man begging at the door may be your neighbour but not the people in the Third World whose fate may be slightly affected depending on your vote at the next election.

This theology, which locates the God-experience in the consciousness of the individual who has despaired of society, is the form that Christianity takes when we accept the *cultus privatus* theory of religion. The God-experience is permitted to make a difference to us and to the people we meet, at least if we can create I-and-thou situations of spontaneous intimacy; but it makes no difference whatever to our situation in its totality as social-political and industrial-commercial. This form of Christianity, for all its rhetoric of being radical and existential, for all its talk of encounter and decision, is not a faith that the world is ever going to hate (John 15, 19; 17, 14). It is a faith that makes not the slightest difference to anything, outside the circle of one's immediate friends. Nobody is going to challenge this faith, it is too private to make enough difference to anybody for him to react to it at all, far less to react hostilely. Privatized like this, the God-experience is irrelevant, it has nothing to do with society at all.

The second form of Christianity which Moltmann detects and denounces is what he calls the cult of *Mitmenschlichkeit*. This conception has its roots deep in the original Romantic reaction against the new industrial society, and the characteristic formula is the distinction between community and society, between *Gemeinschaft* and *Gesellschaft*. Society is the organization it takes to run a great industrial conurbation, while community is where we meet face to face as persons. This is an ideal of community which can play an important critical and therapeutic role in humanizing society; but it is also very easy to slide into abandoning the struggle to reconstruct society. It is easy, Moltmann suggests, to romanticize the local church-community into a refuge from the anonymous, faceless society. Here, in the limited group, you can have all the human warmth and seriousness, the genuine community, which the conditions of modern society make impossible. The Church can be a kind of Noah's ark for us in our alienation from society; in the great sea of structures and relationships which one can do nothing whatever to change, one can have these islands of fellowship and authentic humanity. You can change nothing in the brutal facts of how all that is truly human is being annihilated in modern society, you can merely provide sanctuary, so that people can endure the horrors of modern society on the strength of occasional withdrawal into genuine community.

This is the idea that the Church only happens in the interstices of society, in the holes where we take shelter. That the God-experience does occur in such

privileged community-situations need not be denied:
it is surely what Karl Rahner's diaspora ecclesiology
involves. The point is to ensure that the experience of
true community is not merely a refuge from the pressures of society but a stance of protest and critique
against structures that prevent the diffusion of this
experience.

The third posture which Christianity takes up in
our society is what Moltmann calls the cult of the
institution. So much of our life is institutionalized that it
seems appropriate that the Church should regain, or
retain, its function as the institution which ultimately
guarantees the status quo, the stability, the sense of
security, which so much institutionalization creates,
or is supposed to create. Christianity in this case becomes part of the milieu, not only not changing anything but actually confirming and conniving with the
existing order of things, whatever it may be in any
particular situation.

Granted, then, that there is this tension now between the social-political-structural-institutional and the
individual-personal dimensions of human life, we
can see that each of these three postures which the
Church takes up in our society, really evades the
burden of bearing or reconciling this tension. The first
two opt out of it by writing off the social-structural
side of life by saying that there is nothing one can do
about it. Either you must withdraw into the privacy of
your own subjectivity, to preserve *that,* or you must
withdraw with your friends to create some oasis of
genuine community, in the face of the pressures of the
anonymous society. The third possibility is to refuse
the strain by simply continuing the traditional ecclesiastical role of sanctioning and sacralizing the existing

public order, to allow the Church to be a stabilizing institution among all the other stabilizing institutions (don't rock the boat).

All of these are postures which the Church is put into by modern society. But Moltmann's point is that the believing community cannot acquiesce in any roles forced upon it or demanded of it by modern society. The Church must choose its own role in society; or rather, the Church must fulfil the mission demanded of it by God.

Faith, hope and charity is how our God-experience happens: it is charity and the other theological virtues by which the human heart is put into relationship with God (St Thomas Aquinas, *Summa,* Ia, IIae, Q. 68, 8; IIa, IIae, Q. 151, 2). How our relationship to God happens, if it happens at all, is what we call faith, hope and charity. To write a 'theology of hope' is to write a theology of our 'experience of God.' Of course Christians have an 'experience of God': it is what we speak of in terms of faith, hope, and charity.

We may assume that the God who has raised our hopes expects more of us than modern society does. Our relationship to modern society will be fruitful, as Moltmann says, only if it is conflict-laden. It is only where our resistance, our refusal to be adapted and neutralized in one way or another, shows us up as a group which cannot be assimilated, that we can begin to communicate our hope to society. The believing community in its common hope must be a source of permanent unrest and disturbance in society, which nothing can silence or allay or accommodate. And this will not happen, Moltmann argues, if all our challenging is done in ways in which the public-social-structural dimension of human life is left intact.

It is precisely by breaking the status quo, by breaking the silence in which the assumptions of our society are carefully kept, that we make our presence felt as people with an eschatology. It is true that when theologians and preachers speak of eschatology our hearts sink: eschatology seems to have no application anywhere, at best it sounds like poetry, at worst like theological verbalizing; but in fact, of course, far from being something nebulous and transcendental and unsubstantial, eschatology is precisely what is practicable, creative, productive, constructive and relevant in our God-experience, if anything is. Christianity *is* eschatology; our God-experience is nothing if it is not the sense of the claim on us of the eschaton and the promise to us of the future; and it is this, precisely, which must make us permanently dissatisfied with any existing or imaginable social order.

It is our eschatology which must make us keep asking awkward questions—but to be awkward our questions must be heard and then answered not in the sanctuary of the individual conscience only, not out on the fringes of society where groups have opted out, but at the centre of society. The question which the God-people have to put to the world, the hope which the God-people bear to the world, is not for this or that individual or for any fringe group but for the world as a whole, for society as a whole. The question we have to put and the hope we have to bear, as the God-people, can never be private. The God-experience which is faith, hope and charity, can in fact be neither the state religion of the Roman Empire or of the Lyndon Johnson empire nor the private religion of any world-weary élite group. Our God-experience cannot be either the *cultus publicus* or a *cultus privatus* in any existing or imaginable social order. Christianity is both public and private or it is nothing.

It is because Christianity is eschatology that Christianity is politics, in the sense in which politics means the whole area to do with the *polis,* the city, the human community (which need not necessarily always mean party-politics: in many situations it is possible that involvement in party-politics is just a mystificatory evasion of real involvement in total politics). If Christianity is relevant to society it is not in spite of the eschatology but precisely because of the fact that Christianity is eschatology. It is as eschatology that Christianity becomes politics (in the sense defined). Christian eschatology occurs as politics.

Lumen Gentium §35: 'We show ourselves children of the promise when, strong in faith and hope, we redeem the present time and look forward in patience to future glory. But we must not conceal this hope in the depths of our hearts but on the contrary express it through the structures of ordinary secular life, in permanent conversion and in conflict with the rulers of the world of this darkness, the spirits of unrighteousness.'

If the Church is to be the Church-for-the-world, this cannot mean that the Church must be the Church which the world wants, or even the Church such as the world will allow it to be. It has to be the Church with its mission to the world, to society, happening all the time in the context of the expectation of the coming of the kingdom of God, not in the context of the social roles which society may expect of it or impose upon it. The Church is not for the world in the sense of preserving the world and of maintaining the status quo . . . 'The Christian Church is not supposed to serve mankind so that this world may remain exactly what it is; on the contrary, the Church is supposed to serve mankind so that the world, society, may be transformed and become what it has been promised.'

For the believing community, the gospel which Jesus preached and which we now preach in proclaiming his resurrection from the dead, is that the rule of God has broken in upon us and that this means that our whole perspective and prospect has changed. We must see ourselves in a totally new light, in the light of the resurrection of Jesus, and this means that, far from being able to put up with ourselves and the existing order of things, whatever they may be in any particular instance, we can no longer put up with ourselves as we are, our past selves, or with things as they are, the structures of this world. We must always be seeking to surpass them, to change them, in view of what is to come.

Moltmann rightly takes up, at this point, the full biblical sense of salvation (*yesha,* deliverance, liberation), and insists that it is no mere rescuing of the individual soul from this wicked world but on the contrary the hope of righteousness, *tsedaqa:* the righteousness of God which occurs as right relationships in the human community. How the present is affected by the future is in our hope in *tsedaqa*. Jesus has been raised for our *tsedaqa* (Romans 4, 25), the city of *tsedaqa* (Isaiah I, 26). The kingdom of God hasn't to do only with individuals; the *tsedaqa* of the promised future is a community. Refusing to conform to the principles of this society doesn't mean personal conversion in the sense of just becoming different inside yourself, it means changing the structure of the whole society in which one's God-experience occurs

. . . changing it in opposition to it and in creative expectation of its future, the future which God has promised. It is precisely the relationships that exist here and now among men and between men and things that those who have had the God-experience in Christ cannot stand any longer. As Moltmann says, we simply cannot put up with the status quo, we must constantly seek to shift all social institutions out of their tendency to stabilize and rigidify, to unsettle them, to open them again and again to the pressure of the future: 'in constructive opposition and in creative reshaping, Christian hope puts the existing state of things, things as they are, into question, and in this way prepares the way for what is to come . . . set as it is on the new situation which is always expected, Christian hope is always transcending the existing situation, whatever it is, seeking opportunities to correspond more and more to the future in history which has been promised.'

Moltmann launches out into a severe attack on the trad·tional Lutheran conception of the Christian vocation as merely doing one's duty within society. Merely keeping things going as they are could never be the Christian vocation. 'Creative discipleship' (a phrase from Ernst Wolf) cannot consist in adjusting to and conserving the existing social and political order, whatever it may be, still less in giving it religious backing. The key phrase is, however, from Ernst Bloch, the unorthodox Marxist philosopher on whose work Moltmann leans heavily for inspiration: 'creative expectation', *schöpferische Erwartung*. Christianity is eschatology, Christianity is hope, Christianity is expectation; and expectation which inaugurates and stimulates critique and transformation of the existing order of things, whatever it may be, in view of the city of righteousness, the true human community, which God has promised in the resurrection of Jesus—the promise that self-sacrifice for others prevails in the end, despite all the evidence to the contrary, over violence and hatred.

Eschatology occurs as politics. If you get some idea of the community offered in the promise God has made, then you must be shocked by any existing or imaginable social-political order. You must find yourself protesting and criticizing. Your eschatology, if you take it seriously, is inevitably a stance from which to criticize any existing order of things; it is bound to bring you into permanent conflict with much of what you see around you. There would be something wrong with believers who found nothing to protest against in their social-political situation; this would mean that their eschatology had become ineffective, that their hope in the future God has promised must be weak. Eschatology is the sense of community which God has promised to us; if we really hope in this, our experience of the *polis* as it is here and now must be subjected to radical critique and reconstruction. It is difficult to suppose that the creative-critical role which Christian eschatology might play in politics has ever been more persuasively described than it is in *Theology of Hope*.

NOTES

1. *Theology of Hope*, by Jürgen Moltmann, S.C.M. Press, 1967, 45f.
2. Cf. "Priesthood and Ministry," by Cornelius Ernst, O.P., *New Blackfriars*, December 1967, especially p. 131.
3. Cf. "Secular Christianity," by Brian Wicker, *New Blackfriars*, May 1966.

GREGORY BAUM

The Future at Brussels

THE IMPORTANCE OF THE Congress did not lie in
the approved propositions. Of greater significance were
the conversations among theologians, during the working sessions and in private, which brought out their
personal views on the issues raised by the speakers or
on other matters that especially concerned them. In
these conversations a learning process took place. Here
theologians gained new insight, found some correction,
had their own views confirmed, and were instilled with
a stronger desire to dedicate themselves to research
and reflection.

In this article I wish to describe three important
theological themes expressed in several papers and in
many discussions at the Congress even if they only
affected incidentally the final resolutions.

1. *There was a general willingness on the part of
theologians to recognize the growing non-conformism
in the Catholic Church.* Even Yves Congar, the greatest
and most original of classical ecclesiologists and the
unofficial creator of Vatican II's vision of the Church,

* Father Gregory Baum, noted theologian, is editor
of *The Ecumenist* and the author of numerous articles and
books. His latest book is *Man Becoming*. The International
Congress of Theology, organized by the publishers of
Concilium, brought 220 theologians to Brussels in Sep-
tember 1970. This is a slightly condensed report of significant themes discussed.

admitted in his paper that the presence of Catholics in the Church, who cannot identify themselves with all of Catholic teaching and do not wish to follow the entire ecclesiastical legislation, must be taken seriously in a theological understanding of the Church. They belong to the Church, and the theologian must render an account of how they do belong. Yves Congar, in line with more traditional concepts, referred to these people, often the intellectual elite of the community, as marginal Catholics. As the Synagogue of the first century was surrounded by pious pagans who participated in the faith of Israel without following the Law, and as the early Church was often surrounded by catechumens who though believers in Christ were unable or unwilling to be baptized, so, according to Père Congar, the Catholic Church, defined by its teaching and its law, embraces Catholics who participate in its basic faith without being able to accept the Church in its entirety. They must be respected, Père Congar argued; they have a proper ecclesiological status.

Congar's analysis was not accepted by all theologians. In what sense are the non-comformist Catholics "marginal"? Must one not try to understand their presence in terms of the change, theological and social, that is taking place in the Catholic Church? The nonconformist Catholics in the first part of the 20th century disagreed with the Papacy and common ecclesiastical opinion on religious liberty, on the importance of the vernacular in the liturgy, on the need for ecumenism and an open attitude to the world, on dialogue with other religions and on the dignity and the rights of personal conscience. Yet, they were not marginal to the Church, they constituted the spiritual and intellectual source for the Church's development at Vatican II in the second half of the 20th century. There may indeed be some non-conformists who are marginal, who are prevented by inner or outer obstacles from accepting the fullness of revealed truth, but the experience of the last decades has convinced us that there are other non-conformists, who have a profound grasp of Christian truth and anticipate the Church's doctrinal and social development, and who must, therefore, be regarded at the Church's creative frontier. Many, if not most, of the theologians gathered at Brussels disagreed with various aspects of the teaching and the legislation presently entertained by the ecclesiastical government: yet, they did not think of themselves as marginal.

In my own paper read to the Congress, I analyzed the situation of a great number of Catholics who are unable to identify themselves unconditionally with the ecclesiastical system. While they are committed to the mystery of redemption, proclaimed and celebrated in the Church, they realize that the ecclesiastical system is not an absolute. They look forward to changes in ecclesiastical law and structure and anticipate the reinterpretation of traditional dogma in the light of the Church's present experience. They put brackets around the elements of the Catholic system that do not make sense to them or contradict, in their view, the more central Catholic positions on faith, hope and charity.

Among the educated, these people are the rule. While they may number among them the half-hearted, they also include the creative minds of the Church and the truly sensitive Christians who are the source of the Church's renewal. Though these non-conformist Catholics are not acknowledged in the official propositions of the Congress, it was my impression that the theologians took their existence for granted and assigned them a role, in some cases even a crucial role, in the life of the Church.

These non-conformist Catholics are in need of special pastoral care. The Congress did not deal with this. Catholics who find that they must disagree with some aspects of official Catholicism, may lack the theological training to put their convictions into words, engage in fruitful conversation with others, and in this manner remain in the Christian community. In some places the negative attitude of the ecclesiastical hierarchy may intensify their alienation. What was at first a creative frontier of Catholic life for them may thus become an open door through which they pass out of the Christian community altogether. There is need to explain to non-conformist Catholics the peculiar, historical or developmental nature of the Church so that by looking at the Catholic Church in the present stage of transition, they find their own place in it, as well as a place for the more traditionally-minded Catholics.

2. *The Congress dealt at some length with an important theme, closely connected with non-conformist Catholicism, namely that of theological pluralism.* From various points of view, this pluralism was examined by the special speakers. Edward Schillebeeckx studied it in some detail in his paper. The final propositions approved by the Congress explicitly acknowledge theological pluralism in the Church.

The plurality of theology is derived first of all from the various philosophies and other systems of thought, which are employed in expressing and explaining the Christian message. While the ancient fathers of the Church drew upon Plato and Plotinus and the theologians of the 13th century made use of

Aristotelian philosophy, contemporary theology is in dialogue with phenomenology, existentialism, and other systems in order to put into words and concepts the Good News revealed in Jesus Christ. Today in particular theology is also in conversation with the social sciences. If divine revelation in Jesus Christ creates the new man or the new humanity, then the categories drawn from psychology and sociology may be useful and even necessary for understanding and putting into words the message of redemption for today. Pluralism in theology means that the same Christ proclaimed by the Church can be spoken of and explained within various frames of reference.

Yet, theological pluralism goes deeper than manifold forms for the identical Christian message. Since the Christian message addresses man in concrete historical situations, i.e. reveals to him the sin from which he suffers and offers him forms of new, redeemed life, this message is not identical in every age and every situation, except in the deepest sense of being summed up in the person of Jesus Christ. This pluralism in the Christian message we see already in the New Testament. The content of the Good News, as addressed to a Jewish audience with its Biblical background, was quite different from that addressed to an audience of people with no link to the Biblical tradition. To them both the threats to human existence and the possibility of new life were presented in a manner derived from their own experience of reality. The formulation of the Christian message is, in part at least, a function of the culture in which the Church lives. In order to make the Christian message the Good News for contemporary society, the Church must again and again reinterpret it. The history of this reinterpreta-

tion, Catholics call "tradition." The traditioning of the
Gospel is a creative thing, not a mere repetition of
the ancient creeds, but a new grasp, produced by
the Spirit, on the redemptive thrust of the Gospel in the
present, making known the present form of sin and
destruction and the present possibilities of freedom
and grace.

The theological pluralism in the Church makes it
very difficult indeed to define what its doctrinal unity
means. The Congress did not deal with this important
question. The special papers and the approved propositions dealing with the Christian message simply say
that the Christian message must always be linked to
the person of Christ, that in its formulation the ancient
creeds retain their significance, but that there is need
today for reinterpretation and reformulation. This
leaves a lot of leeway.

It is at this point that conservative and progressive
theologians begin to differ. Conservative theologians
want to preserve the self-identity of the Christian message by making it conform as much as possible to the
ancient creeds, while progressive theologians want to
preserve the self-identity of this message by formulat-
ing it as the Good News for today. The latter hold that
the self-identity cannot be preserved by repeating the
old formulas, for today these formulas no longer reveal
to people the sin that devours them or the grace that
restores them. The Christian message can only be
preserved intact if it remains Good News. What is being
passed on in the Church is not a set of concepts, a
conceptual analysis of God and His self-manifestation
in Christ, but a message that communicates new life,
a message in which God reveals the powers of man's
undoing and the grace, offered to him, by which new

vitality becomes available to him. The Congress dealt with this question only indirectly. Stressing the need for reformulating the message, it favored the progressive trend in the Church, but the somewhat narrow Christological emphasis in some of the propositions seemed to favor the conservative trend.

In the treatment of theological pluralism and the meaning of the Christian message, a point was made several times which, though never moving to the center of attention, eventually found expression in the final propositions. Man's intellectual achievement and his view of reality are never wholly unrelated to the way in which he lives, privately and politically. Thus, the utterance of Christian truth and its theological formulation always reflect the actual situation in which Christians and the Church find themselves. The Congress adopted the view, first made by Marx, though in a reductionist sense, that positions adopted by the Church inevitably reflect the social involvement of the Church, financially and politically, and that, therefore, all striving after orthodoxy and Christian truth must be based on a more fundamental search for *orthopraxis,* i.e. for the style of life, personal and social, that is in harmony with Christ and His message. If we live in patterns that are wholly unevangelical, we cannot lay hold of the Gospel and express it adequately.

By relating the style of life and the institutional involvement of people to theology and the formulation of the Christian message, the Congress touched upon an important point of critique, still quite undeveloped, which puts into question the highly academic and conceptual approach to theology characteristic of many centuries of church history. If it is true, as Maurice Blondel always insisted, that we can know only what we do, the renewal of theology is not simply an intellectual quest but a more total involvement of Christians in finding life styles and forms of community life that embodies more closely the spirit of Christ.

3. *What will be the institutional or structural reality of the Church in the future?* Several papers were given on this topic. All agreed that the New Testament leaves the widest possible margin for future developments. In the New Testament a structure is called divine, or created by the Spirit, if it serves the needs of the community. God is present to the community in this ministry. The highly centralized ministry that has developed in the West and climaxed in the Papacy is understood by Catholics as a Spirit-guided development, even though they see in it also a reflection of human sin. The propositions approved by the Congress affirm that the Church's divine structure allows developments of all kinds. What is needed today, these propositions say, is the introduction of new ecclesiastical processes which permit more participation in teaching and policy-making on the part of Christians everywhere.

Yet, a democratization of the ecclesiastical structure alone will not help. What is more important is the social renewal of Christian life from below. We have to create new matrices of Christian life in the world. Will the parish structure do? Is the diocese really a reflection of how the Spirit groups the Christian people today? Many speakers made a demand, which was eventually adopted in one of the propositions, that the Church should encourage the creation of small groups. It should be possible to reconstitute the Christian people, not around pre-fabricated structures, but around common interests, concerns, and issues and thus facilitate the creation of small communities with their own proper role in the Church. The structure of the Church could be made to follow the action of the Spirit, i.e. it could integrate in conversation and cooperation the groups and communities which in fact crystallize in the Christian people.

At the moment the structure of the Catholic Church is still that of an empire with many provinces. The question posed by the Congress is whether this Church could not become instead a world-wide movement of cells. These cells are created by people as they are touched by the Spirit. This would make the Church into a grass-roots movement, provide multiple patterns of Christian life, and enable Catholics to participate in the Church's life on their own responsible terms. Only an institutional change of such magnitude could adapt the episcopo-papal system to the needs of the present. It would enable the non-conformist Catholics to form living cells in the movement, it would provide a unitary pattern for theological pluralism, it would empower the Church to be forever in a state of transition, from one age to the next, even if the rate of change is different in different cells. The Church as a movement of cells would solve the ecumenical problem and might even encourage the formation of tightly-bound small communities, be they technically "religious" or not, who live as a single family and adopt a style of life that offers a viable alternative to modern urban existence.

In the discussion of the three themes, the existence of non-conformist Catholics, the pluralism of theology and the Church restructured as movement, the international Congress held at Brussels may indeed be prophetic for the future development of the Catholic Church.

CARDINAL LEO SUENENS

After Vatican II

VATICAN II ALREADY SEEMS far away. At a recent meeting of the French hierarchy, where memories of the council were evoked, a newly appointed bishop was heard to remark: "The elders speak of Verdun! (major indecisive battle of World War I)."

Whether we like it or not, Vatican II is already history, and that means the past. By that very fact, certain traits appear today as marked by time and show their inevitable limitations.

A council is the work of men through whom the Holy Spirit acts. But where men are at work, it is very normal that purely human factors intervene and leave their mark.

This historical relativity of Vatican II is clearly seen in these four directions:

1. Completely new problems appeared after Vatican II and became the problems of the day in all research and discussion. I think, for example, of contemporary atheism and all the literature on the "Theology of the Death of God."

* Cardinal Leo Suenens of Belgium was one of the major figures in the Vatican Council of 1962–1965. Since the Council, Cardinal Suenens has been a strong supporter of co-responsibility in the Church and has suggested various steps for modernizing the structure of the Roman Curia. In this article, he looks at the state of things in the Church half a decade after the Council.

2. We are much more aware today that certain problems were only half-solved. At the recent World Congress of Theologians in Brussels, I pressed the theologians present to make an ever deeper study of some of these. For example:

The synthesis between the hierarchical and the charismatical element in and of the Church;

The harmony between Tradition and Scripture as source of Revelation;

The exact meaning and significance of what the council termed a "hierarchy of truths." This could be of incalculable ecumenical importance.

3. It is evident today that a certain number of happy initatives taken by the council for the government of the Church have not yet been fully exploited. I am thinking especially of what the Roman Synod could become if the present rule was revised so as to make it an instrument of authentic collegiality.

I think also of the councils of priests and of pastoral councils, their complementarity and interplay and all the hope they contain for the future if they are seriously implemented.

We could apply here the following words of Pope Paul VI: "The conciliar decrees are not so much a destination as a point of departure towards new goals . . . The seeds of life planted by the Council in the soil of the Church must grow and achieve full maturity."

4. Finally there is an internal logic in Vatican II which in several cases has been grasped and acted on, showing in everyday practice the priority of life over law. The spirit behind the texts was stronger than the words themselves.

We can see this in the liturgical reform, widespread in the Church today. And yet at the council, how many restrictive clauses got into the decree!

See also how that very vague invitation of the council to cardinals and bishops to retire was made practical politics by the Pope himself when he started the curial reform and decreed that prelates should normally retire from office at the age of 75.

All this shows that Vatican II is only a stage, not a terminus, in the history of our time. We see here very closely that the Church is ever a pilgrim people, always on the roads, and that it cannot afford the luxury of pitching its tent and camping in the same site once and for all.

But this does not diminish in any way the tremendous grace of the council. To all it was evident that the Holy Spirit was at work.

December 1965 saw the end of an era, and the start of another. Vatican II was, in a very special way, a council of transition.

It is not surprising that Vatican II has not been received in the same way by all Christians—and this because of the depth of the reforms it inaugurated and their novelty.

The measure of acceptance of a council is an important element in judging its influence and significance. The Oriental Church has always attached the greatest importance to this acceptance of conciliar decrees by the faithful. It is not possible here to make a theological analysis of this; we simply state a sociological fact.

During these last few years, different sorts of reactions have become apparent. I know that classification easily becomes oversimplification and that real people don't fit into prefabricated categories. A conservative in theology may be a progressive in the pastoral fields or vice versa, but this being said, we can discern three definite tendencies in the members of the Church today.

First of all there are those for whom Vatican II was a simple parenthesis. As a whole they form the traditionalist, conservative group. They suffer, and rightly so, to see all around the decline in faith and religious practices; the extravagances of certain ultra-progressives hurt them to the quick.

But on the other hand they suffer also for unfounded reasons: they do not distinguish authentic and sacred tradition from purely human traditions accumulated through the ages and which periodically have to be questioned. They believe too easily that real values are being denied where, as more often, they are being simply adapted to our times. They ignore history, and through lack of perspective easily "canonize" a certain past.

At the other extreme, we have a class of exaggerated progressives who reject tradition, who are up in arms against the Church in her institutional elements. In their intemperance to get rid of all organization they risk throwing out the baby with the bath! The Church will never be a welfare association, a sort of spiritual Red Cross. Christ founded her as an institution and a community. Charisms and hierarchy are not mutually exclusive but complementary.

Conservatives are confusing Tradition and traditions. Progressives are confusing liberty and anarchy. Their disregard for continuity with the past could easily lead them to offer the world a Christianity without Christ.

Between these extremes we have to try to keep the middle of the road, the "extreme center."

Tensions are part of humanity and the primitive Church had more than its share, but we must try to lessen them every day. This effort to harmonize different mentalities, to bridge the generation gap, will need patience, moderation, humor and a sense of relativity where non-essentials are concerned. We have to ever aim at being one but to face together, as Christians, the future which is facing us.

To make the future, we must trust that future and understand the new generation, with all their problems, their allergies, their aspirations, their failings. It is with them that we have to construct the future.

Vatican II gave us a new image of the Church and her role for and in the world.

Consequently the role that each individual member is called upon to fulfill must be adapted to this new image. And this adaptation is on the way, but will need more than five years.

It is easy to foresee that, in the years to come, there will be a new style of life, a new way of being a layman, a deacon, a religious, a priest, a bishop and a pope.

All this will not be easily accomplished. Now life is always paid for with the pangs of childbirth. But the real world is always a mixture of light and darkness, like a picture of Rembrandt. And we are sons of light, which means we are by vocation optimists.

Pope John said one day: "I have never seen a pessimist doing useful work for the world." This is Christian and human wisdom.

We have to face the future knowing that the Holy

Spirit is there and that he is a Creating Spirit. We must not be afraid of a new Christianity as long as it is His work.

Where are we going?

Will the next chapter of the Church bring us a Vatican III, with observers from other Christian churches just listening with sympathy? Or will it be some sort of Jerusalem II, an ecumenical council in the universal sense of the word, with no "observers" but only Christians searching together for visible unity?

We do not know. But we know that it is with faith and hope that we must advance on the road toward the third millennium of the Church.